Scania 112 & 142 at work

Patrick W Dyer

Old Pond
PUBLISHING LTD

ACKNOWLEDGEMENTS

My grateful thanks to the following for their help and support: Clive Burnet, Per-Erik Nordström, Kjell Engman Lundberg, Hans-Ake Danielsson, Mikael Person, Del Roll, Adrian Cypher, Marcus Lester, David Wakefield, Clive Davis, John Woods Henderson, Peter Davison, Paul Willis, Steve Lynch, Ashley Coghill, *Commercial Motor*, all at Old Pond and, of course, Linda and Jess Dyer

ABOUT THE AUTHOR

Patrick Dyer, born in 1968, grew up during one of the most notable and exciting periods of development for heavy trucks and the last of the real glory days for trucking as an industry. This is reflected in his subject matter. Previously published in his growing 'Trucks at Work' series are: Scania's LB110, 111 and 141; DAF's 2800, 3300 and 3600; Ford's Transcontinental; Volvo's F88 and F89, followed by the F10 and F12; Seddon Atkinson's 400, 401 and 4-11.

Although Patrick's day job is in motor sports, he holds a Class One licence and drives whenever the opportunity arises. He is also the proud owner of a 1983 Volvo F12, finished in the livery of Edwin Shirley Trucking.

DECLARATION

There were at least six recognised methods of measuring engine output for trucks during the period covered by this book. Manufacturers and magazines often quoted different outputs for the same engine using BS.Au, SAE, DIN and ISO systems, some gross and some net, much to everyone's confusion. Therefore, for clarity, only the figures quoted by Volvo at the time are used throughout this work.

DEDICATION

I would like to dedicate this book to the memory of Edwin Shirley, a visionary of the road haulage and entertainment industries!

ISBN 978-1-908397-87-4

A catalogue record for this book is available from the British Library

Published by
Old Pond Publishing Ltd
Dencora Business Centre,
36 White House Road
Ipswich IP1 5LT
United Kingdom

www.oldpond.com

Front cover photograph
Andy Vane's black R112 was beautifully finished and a credit to the Kent haulier who ran a small fleet of 2-series tractors from his Kent base in the 1980s. Note the neat chassis locker, an item specially developed for this location on the 6 x 2 chassis, which was mirrored on the offside with an identical item. *(Photo: Paul Willis)*

Back cover photograph
Harvester Giant was a late model 2-series heavy haulage tractor employed by H C Wilson. As part of the extensive modular system, the E chassis with double drive and hub reduction axles gave operators a 150-ton capability from standard components. This meant a short lead times for new trucks as no 'special build' was required at the factory. *(Photo: Adrian Cypher)*

Cover design and book layout by Liz Whatling
Printed in China

Contents

Foreword

By Per-Erik Nordström
Head of Product Affairs, Scania, 1994–2013

The model of modules

Employed by Scania in 1976 as editor of operators' manuals, yours truly soon got involved in developing a new generation of service literature aimed for the GPRT truck range to be launched in 1981. In a group of creative colleagues, we explored all nooks and crannies of the new truck range and the far-reaching modularisation and – lo and behold – it turned out that we could modularise the literature as well, gathering the workshop information in booklets instead of large volumes of paper sheets that risked never being looked at. This operators' manual could be tailored with a set of booklets to suit the spec of each individual truck.

The Scania 2-series meant a breakthrough for modular thinking in the truck industry. Launched as the GPRT-range in 1981, it comprised a vast range of forward-control and bonneted heavy trucks in a multitude of configurations for all types of heavy truck applications. The 2-series was conceived from the outset to suit all imaginable customer applications and share as many parts and components as possible without any compromises in functionality.

The concept of a fully modularised truck range matured and was tried out full scale on Scania's V8 trucks in the 140 and 141-series during the 1970s. The legendary LB 140 4x2, LBS 140 6x2 and LBT 140 6x4 introduced in 1969 were followed by bonneted models in 1972 – L 140 4x2, LS 140 6x2 and the LT 145 6x4. The latter featured a heavy-duty chassis, hence the digit 5 in the designation.

This V8 family of vehicles was built using the concept that would form the basis for GPRT. Modularisation meant that the chassis design was identical on forward-control and bonneted models. All components except the cab remained in the same positions, with identical mounting points. The fully modularised truck concept thus underwent trials for a full decade before GPRT emerged.

Takes a long time to mature

Scania's philosophy of modular product design goes all the way back to the Scania-Vabis 'Royal' unitary diesel engine launched in 1939 in 4- and 6-cylinder versions for use in trucks. In the early 1950s they were followed by an 8-cylinder unit fitted to railcars and, transversely-mounted, powering the remarkable Scania-Vabis Metropol suburban bus, which was based on a rear-engine Mack design.

Modularisation gradually extended to other systems and components and became visually evident with the launch of the new 80 and 110 models in 1968. Less visible, but equally clever, were the identical chassis of the bonneted and forward-control V8 models. The smaller bonneted L, LS and LT models continued in the design presented in 1958 until replaced by GPRT in 1981.

Graduation time

The GPRT range was thus the mature result of Scania-Vabis' modular design philosophy, which permeated all aspects of the trucks. The modular chassis frame was available in three strength classes and various strength ratings were available for axles and gearboxes.

The sharp Giugiaro styling pioneered a trend towards more homogeneous truck styling in Europe – nothing wrong in them looking good. The cab panels and doors were styled in modules that could be cut to the right height and length. The additional cooler required for the charge-cooling introduced in 1982 required some extra space, so the grille moved forward a few centimetres. With new corner sections, this actually improved the styling. The angular plastic bonnet neatly blended with the cab shape.

The basic cab design was contemporary, yet aged well into the 3-series in 1988 and subsequently the Scania Streamline launched in conjunction with Scania's centenary celebrations in 1991.

A remarkable feat was the transition to the new range in Latin America, which only took four months. With production in Sweden, the Netherlands, Brazil and Argentina and assembly in several other countries, Scania's new modular truck range was truly a global product that was at the forefront of truck design. Buses and coaches followed suit a couple of years later, using much the same philosophy in the design of chassis modules.

A matter of clever interfaces

For Scania, the modular philosophy goes considerably deeper than mere standardisation. The crucial point is the design of interfaces between components, which allows components of different strengths to be combined in innumerable ways. This work cannot be done overnight. Systems and components need to be designed to fit together long in advance. Creative

thinking along these lines started in the early 1950s, but it was only realistic to take the step to modularise the LB and L 140 two decades later. A further 10 years on, in 1981, the concept was implemented to the full on GPRT.

A low-output engine in a heavy-duty chassis, linked to a heavy-duty transmission makes for an unburstably robust construction vehicle. A powerful engine in a medium-duty chassis will provide a fast, light and economical long-haulage vehicle.

At the time of the GPRT launch, Scania management estimated the total number of possible spec combinations to be approaching 2 billion, counting everything from cabs down to tyres and brackets. In more conventional terms, the number of different truck models was around 300, ignoring variations in engine output, cab size, wheelbase, etc.

Modularisation sounds simple, but required several decades to mature into a marketable concept. Competitors have naturally looked hard at Scania's philosophy and are still striving to catch up.

Per-Erik Nordström
February 2014

5

Meet the ancestors

By 1980, from the sum of its parts Scania could claim nearly ninety years of vehicle production of one sort or another. Vabis, the older of the two original companies, was founded in 1891 initially to build rolling stock for the railways, but diversified as early as 1897 when it built Sweden's first motor car. Scania, originally a bicycle manufacturer – from where the company's sprocket logo would emerge – was only a few years behind Vabis in producing a motorised vehicle of its own. The two companies joined forces in 1911 bringing together their individual experience of commercial vehicle manufacture. In 1968 Saab was added to the equation. At the time Saab was a fledgling car manufacturer with just nineteen years of automotive production behind it, but it had been building aircraft since 1937 and, like any successful company in the aerospace industry, was a full of the bright ideas many of which would ultimately filter through to truck design in one shape or another. By the mid 1970s, Saab-Scania (the Vabis name had been dropped from the title by then) was employing over 40,000 people, which was large for a Swedish company at the time. Through its various

Scania's modern era of forward control trucks and its rise to international prominence started right here. The remarkable LB76 with its 11-litre engine was an instant hit with hauliers and it proved the perfect truck for the emerging TIR routes due to its power plus reliability, comfort and safety. The company's annual production figures grew significantly in the years following its 1963 debut and reached 11,000 vehicles in 1966, nearly 5,000 more than at the start of the decade. Although the cab was fixed, the LB76 was equipped with a large swing-out radiator, which did much to improve servicing. The model stayed in production until 1968. (Photo: Scania AB)

divisions it was involved in the manufacture of cars, trucks, buses, aircraft, missiles, valves, computers and a number of other products.

Although the G P R T range, or 2-series, could justifiably trace its lineage to the L75 of the late 1950s, its most significant ancestor was the remarkable LB76 and its derivatives introduced in 1963. For while the L75 was ground breaking in a few key areas, it was the LB76, a forward control design to meet the changing legislation of mainland Europe and beyond, which really set the mould for Scania's future products.

The LB76 forged a good reputation for Scania at a key time when road haulage was expanding across borders and becoming truly international. This changing industry required trucks with greater performance, reliability and comfort. Mindful of the latter, Scania introduced the LB110 in 1968 with a remarkable new tilt cab to top-off the proven LB76 components. The LB110 also marked the start of Scania's impressive modular system, which allowed the company to build a wide range of trucks to suit a multitude of roles from a

rationalised selection of chassis, engines, gearboxes, axles and cabs. With its stable mates the LB80 and the LB140, Scania could cover the weight categories from 16 to 130 tons and all from a comparatively small number of standard components. It could also produce bonneted versions of the same trucks, the L80, L110 and L140, from the same components including cabs. Steady improvements were made over the years and a major facelift brought the 1-Series into existence between 1974 and 1976, when the forward control range became the LB81, LB111 and LB141.

From 1963 to 1980 the LB ranges did much to popularise the make outside Sweden, especially throughout Europe, which would become an enormous market for the manufacturer. Its LB trucks, though not cheap, won many friends and were particularly favoured by drivers who appreciated the comfort, safety, performance, reliability and style of the trucks.

Top:

Scania's LB110 of 1968 built on the foundations laid by the LB76 and marked the start of a development process that would see Scania through the next two decades. Now equipped with a modern tilting cab, Scania's trucks were the equal of the best in Europe. Development of the cab had taken four years and the result was a rugged high-datum affair that gave the driver a superb, elevated view of the road and a very comfortable environment in which to work and rest. The square design, by Englishman Lionel Sherrow, was modular and allowed for many variants including a sleeper, as here, to be constructed from standard panels. (Photo: Scania AB)

Right:

Scania developed its LB range through the 1970s, introducing the V8-powered LB140 in 1969 and the improved LB111 in 1975. The LB140 caused quite a stir with its big 350 bhp 14-litre V8 engine and set a precedent for the company for powering its top-of-the-range truck with an engine of this configuration. The LB141, with a further developed version of the V8 producing 375 bhp, was introduced in 1976 and stayed in production until replaced by the 142 of the G P R T range. (Photo: Scania AB)

New Program Scania
– T for 2

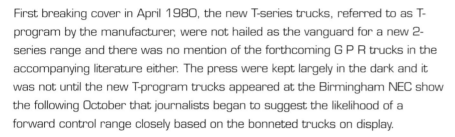

First breaking cover in April 1980, the new T-series trucks, referred to as T-program by the manufacturer, were not hailed as the vanguard for a new 2-series range and there was no mention of the forthcoming G P R trucks in the accompanying literature either. The press were kept largely in the dark and it was not until the new T-program trucks appeared at the Birmingham NEC show the following October that journalists began to suggest the likelihood of a forward control range closely based on the bonneted trucks on display.

However, what was clear from the outset was the further development of Scania's modular build system, which saw the new T-program range introduced as the T82 with 8-litre engine, T112 with 11-litre engine and T142 with 14-litre engine. They all had the same cab and all were available on two common chassis classed M (medium) and H (heavy). Additionally, the 11- and 14-litre trucks were also available with an E chassis (extra heavy-duty).

Despite the familiar mechanical components underneath, there was no disguising the ultra-modern cab/bonnet assembly and Scania made no secret of the fact that it had employed the services of the noted Italian designer, Giorgetto Giugiaro for the project. Not only had Giugiaro made his name penning concept cars like the Maserati Boomerang and road cars such as the original Lotus Esprit and VW Golf, he was also responsible for some stunning furniture designs and had even worked with Nikon on its camera housings. Not since Scammell had employed the services of fellow Italian designer Michelotti for its radical 'cheese grater' cab of the Routeman/Trunker had a truck manufacturer turned to such a high-profile designer.

In a continuation of the theme set with the outgoing bonneted range, the new trucks featured a short-nose conventional design, which was a world away from the long-bonneted offerings of old that had generated the 'torpedo' nickname from which Scania now drew the T prefix for the new range. The results were stunning and although very much in the Scania mould, and instantly recognisable as of its manufacture, the new trucks were bang up to date with a clean, angular design that was not only functional and aerodynamically efficient but aesthetically pleasing too.

On its previous bonneted range, Scania had used the narrower version of its current forward control cab, as fitted to the LB81, as the basis of the crew compartment. For the new T-program trucks, although it would not become truly apparent until the launch of the G P R forward control trucks, it was now fitting a full width one. In fact, in a further move to rationalise parts, Scania would only build the new cab in this one width for the G P R and T-program trucks. As well as giving more space for the crew of the bonneted trucks, this meant that even the most humble of the forward control variants provided the occupants with the same internal width as the top-of-the-range trucks. Comfort was high on the agenda with the new cab, with noise levels coming in for close attention from the design team. The result was a workplace so quiet that some of the original press testers compared it to a Rolls-Royce.

While the T-program was introduced with the existing engines and gearboxes of its predecessors, there were changes made to other driveline components, including axles and prop shafts, to assist the modular concept and further reduce the number of parts required to assemble the different models. As well as streamlining production and reducing the cost of development, the standardisation across the range was also intended to make it easier for customers to identify and order the right truck with the right spec for its intended use. With all those goals in mind Scania succeeded very well indeed.

The T82 replaced the old L81 and provided the entry-level truck for the T-program. As before, Scania's superb DS8 01, 8-litre, 6-cylinder engine, driving through a five- or ten-speed gearbox, was to power it.

Gross weights for the T82 started at 16.24 tons, but this 6 x 2 home-market example was built on the H (heavy) chassis for solo operation at a GVW of 24 tonnes. The lightweight 3-way tipper body by Hiab-Foco was constructed from aluminium and plywood, which allowed a very reasonable 15 tonne payload to be carried. *(Photo: Scania AB)*

As with its equivalent forward control model in the forthcoming G P R range, the T112 filled the middle position in its range, providing vehicles for medium to heavy weight applications and was possibly the most versatile in the T-program. Motive power was from the proven DS11, which in one form or another had powered Scania's 11-litre trucks for twenty years.

Built on the E (extra heavy-duty) chassis, this example was designed for 32-tonne operation in Sweden and, despite its 6 x 4 layout and the heavy mixing drum with its own diesel engine, it could carry an 18.5-tonne load. *(Photo: Scania AB)*

The T142 topped the T-program in fine style with 375 bhp and 1102 lb/ft of torque available from the DS14 06, V8 engine. An example of this configuration, with the 6 x 4 E chassis and 5-speed automatic gearbox with hydraulic torque converter, would have been capable of shifting a 140-tonne load; in fact in this format, the tractor alone was capable of a GVW of 36 tonnes. Yet, while heavy haulage was the T142's forte, it also made a superb long-distance machine if built on the H or M chassis with 6 x 2 or 4 x 2 configuration. This example was fitted with a Eurohitch, extra heavy-duty sliding fifth wheel, which could be raised pneumatically by 530 mm in a vertical plane from the cab. *(Photo: Scania AB)*

The bonnet – which incorporated the wings – of the T-program trucks was originally constructed from reinforced fibre glass, but by the end of 1980 the material was changed to SMC (sheet moulded compound), as used by ERF in the construction of its cabs. The one-piece unit hinged forward to 52 degrees, offering excellent access for servicing. Giugiaro worked a central depression in to the design of the bonnet, his trade mark at the time.

This fine example is fitted with the CT 19 2-birth sleeper cab, but the CT 13 day cab was also available for the T-program trucks and was often classed as '3-man' because it could be fitted with a bench seat for two passengers. Note the neat twin diesel tank installation and dolly, or bonus loader, arrangement employed to haul this high-capacity Noteboom trailer.

(Photo: Scania AB)

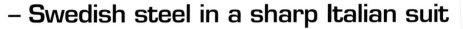

GPR
– Swedish steel in a sharp Italian suit

Scania's new forward control trucks were first shown in December 1980, just nine months behind the introduction of the T-program, following a highly secretive period of final development. At a stroke, the new range replaced all the previous LB forward control trucks. Although developed under the 'Program Scania' banner the new range was to be officially known as 'G P R' after the three cab heights that were to be offered. The G model featured the lowest cab height and was intended for local distribution and municipal roles only. The P model, where the cab was mounted higher, suited a number of applications but in particular tipper work and longer-distance domestic haulage duties. The R model represented the premium end of the range with a high-mounted cab suitable for international TIR haulage with a two-man crew.

As soon as the new trucks emerged it became clear just how thorough Scania had been in rationalising parts and developing its modular system of building trucks. Comparison with the T models revealed that across the board there were common chassis, engines, gearboxes, axles and cabs from which 250 types could be assembled.

The new forward control trucks used exactly the same chassis as the T models with the classification of M, H and E retained. Construction was of constant U-section cold-pressed steel, which, with the exception of the very lightest version of the M chassis, was 9.5 mm thick. For the H and E this was backed up by inner U-section channels of 4 and 8 mm respectively. The outer frames were 270 mm high in all cases with a 70 mm wide flange top and bottom that was of uniform level and pre-drilled to assist the mounting of bodywork. There were standardised cross-member locations throughout all the chassis variants. While still cold-riveted as on previous Scanias, the cross-member brackets were subject to a redesign that increased the width of the base and utilised oval mounting holes to spread load and improve the longevity of the joint. In a move to reduce servicing time and aid fault-finding,

all the air tanks and most of the valves were grouped together on the left of the chassis. The location for the main diesel tank, generally an 88-gallon item, was standardised on the right of the chassis.

In a general move, made in the interest of the better ride characteristics and greater service life, most models were now sprung with parabolic springs manufactured from silico manganese steel. However, traditional multi-leaf set-ups were retained for some of the heavier applications and a rear air suspension system was also made available for specialist applications; indeed, one of the initial Swedish press fleet, a rigid R142M 6 x 2, was so equipped to represent a vehicle suitable for swap body operations.

Front axles were Scania's own AM55 or AM60, of 6,500 kg and 7,000 kg capacity respectively, both manufactured from I-section beam and identical to those used on the old L/LB trucks. Essentially three types of rear axles were offered, though there were variations within each type. These all featured reworked casings, but were, once again, derived from the old L/LB range. They were a lightweight spiral bevel unit, a single reduction hypoid unit and a hub reduction unit, which between them covered everything from light distribution through fast long-distance work to heavy haulage. All but the lightest of the 8-litre M chassis vehicles were available with 6 x 2 and 6 x 4 layouts in addition to 4 x 2. For its 6 x 2 chassis Scania continued with the tried and tested trailing lift axle arrangement.

Gearboxes were either the basic 5-speed G770, the 10-speed GS770 (splitter) or the 10-speed GR870 (range type). Significantly, following a spell of only being offered with the 8-litre engine in the old range, the splitter box was now available behind the 11-litre engine. As before, all three gearboxes were synchromesh units and were direct descendants of those fitted to the L/LB trucks, albeit suitably modified for their new roles. Scania also offered a 5-speed automatic.

During the nine months following the introduction of the T models, Scania did a lot of engine development work on the 8-, 11- and 14-litre units and, with the launch of the G P R range, it introduced new versions of all three engines across the entire range including the bonneted trucks. In a drive to improve fuel efficiency, extend engine life and make driving a quieter and more relaxed experience, Scania further reduced engine speeds and made other changes to increase the torque and power. Key to these improvements were a longer-stroke fuel pump, co-developed with Bosch, which delivered a higher injection rate, a more efficient turbocharger and a new design of cylinder head giving better combustion characteristics. Of the larger engines there were now two variants of the 11-litre unit, the DS11 14 providing 280 bhp and the DS11 15 providing 305 bhp. Both now ran to a new maximum of 2,000 rpm and gave peak torque figures of 860 and 911 lb/ft respectively at 1,300 rpm, an increase of around 11% over the old engines. The re-worked 14-litre V8, now designated the DS14 06, produced 388 bhp and 1,164 lb/ft of torque, enough for Scania to regain the title of 'most powerful truck diesel in Europe'.

With a chassis familiar from the T models, and mechanical components derived from the proven LBs, the most outstanding feature of the new range was the impressive cab designed by Giugiaro, undoubtedly at its most imposing in the towering R version. While the family resemblance to the crew compartment of the T model was plain to see, it was maybe less obvious to the observer that Scania had managed to develop the four cab types for the range (G P R T) from just two versions of the same cab, essentially a day cab and a sleeper. This remarkable feat of design and engineering allowed Scania to reduce the 4,000 parts required to build all the cab variants for the old L/LB ranges to 1,400 for the G P R T. To illustrate the point, the new range required just two roof pressings as opposed to eight. Although not going down the full four-point suspension system as offered by rivals such as Volvo and Ford, Scania did improve

matters greatly over the old LB cab design by incorporating a proper shock and spring system at the rear, which worked in conjunction with rubber mountings at the front. As well as improving comfort for the driver, this system greatly reduced the stresses imposed on the cab structure, especially as the mounts were now moved back for a sleeper cab installation eliminating the previous overhang of the old LB models.

Although Scania could not have engineered it, the 1980 introduction of the new trucks placed the company in a very good position among its competitors. Volvo's F10/12 range was three years old and three years away from its first significant re-development. DAF, although constantly improving its trucks and introducing variants such as the 3300, was eight years away from a truly new range. Mercedes-Benz had its established 'new generation' which would essentially soldier on until 1988. Ford was struggling on with its great, but misunderstood, Transcontinental. Most others, such as Renault, IVECO/FIAT, Bedford, Seddon Atkinson and ERF, were of limited appeal outside of their home countries. In fact, the only rival of concern to Scania that had introduced a new range around the same time was Leyland. Its T45, while potentially very good, was dogged by problems from day one due to the dire state of the company group and never materialised as a threat to Scania's 2-series.

Developments and detail changes to the 2-series were ongoing throughout the production life of the range and most were introduced with little fuss made by the manufacturer. One of the most significant engineering changes, other than the introduction of the intercooled engines that are covered elsewhere, were the improved gearboxes that were available from 1983. This saw the main gearboxes now designated the GR871 and GS871.

The incredible breadth of the modular system and the fact that Scania produced all the major components made the G P R T, or 2-series, the most modern, complete and competitive truck range then available.

Scania carried out a huge study in aerodynamics for the new cab range. Original tests were conducted by the Royal Institute of Technology in Stockholm where 1:10 scale models were evaluated in a wind tunnel. Particular attention was placed on defining the optimum angle of rake for the windscreen and the ideal radii for the cab corners. From these findings Scania delivered a remit to the Italian designer Giugiaro, who then developed the styling for the trucks. His renditions were turned into half-scale models which were secretly shipped to England for testing by the British Motor Industry Research Association (MIRA). All the cab types of G P R and T were tested with various bodywork/loads and aerodynamic aids. The intermediate P cab representation being tested here features an earlier design of roof deflector that was not adopted for production. Note the car on wheels on which the model was built. *(Photo: Scania AB)*

The cab interior came in for equal attention from the design team with the goal of providing the safest and most comfortable Scania yet. Although the T model is shown here, as the modular system employed the same cab across the board it is also representative of the forward control version, too. The only difference inside was the completely flat floor of the T models, which was achievable as there was no intrusion from the mechanical components. In this respect, of the forward control cabs, the high-mounted R version fared best with only a minor intrusion to the floor but this was more marked with the G and P models where it became a genuine engine tunnel.

As well as the cab, chassis and running gear, the modular system was also applied to the dashboard to allow left- and right-hand versions from the same components and the same rationale was applied to pedal holes and similar handed apertures in the cab frame.

All but the very basic interiors, offered only for Third World countries, now featured these superb Bostrum 303 seats as standard, though Scania still insisted in installing them on their own rather unusual base with its rocker mounting system, which some testers and drivers found a little disconcerting in use.

(Photo: Scania AB)

Although the model designations of 82, 112 and 142 as applied to the T-program trucks gave advance notice of the 2-series nomenclature that Scania would apply to the forward control trucks, anyone with a weather eye to the company's bus program would already have spotted the introduction of the BR112 as early as 1978. This bus chassis, based around the normally aspirated version of the 11-litre engine, replaced the similarly powered BR111, which in turn had replaced the BR110.

Although produced after the G P R launch, Laxa manufactured this interesting vehicle utilising some of the cab panels from the range but on a bus chassis. Laxa has a long history of working with Scania on special projects and has been in and out of its direct ownership over the years. As well as featuring a bus/coach chassis, this pantechnicon-style vehicle also sports a 'Scania 112' coach badge. *[Photo: Scania AB]*

While the public had to wait until January 1981 for its official European launch, the press and employees got to see the new trucks first-hand in Sweden late in 1980. To illustrate the scope of the modular system fully, most of the main variants were on display along with examples of the half-scale wind tunnel models. The G82 illustrated on the left was very much the entry-level truck for the range and although it is outside the scope of a book that concentrates on the 112 and 142, it merits inclusion for the fact that, although the range was based on three chassis variants, there were actually four. At entry level, the M chassis was available in two gauges for the side members. For 4 x 2 trucks with a wheelbase of 5.4 m or under, thinner 8 mm thick chassis side members were used instead of the usual 9.5 mm of all others.

Below, the G P R T range in all its glory. This great publicity shot featuring the four elements of the range was often to be found on the back of 2-series brochures and it clearly highlighted the height differences between the trucks. There were several versions of the photo, one featuring a green rather than blue T-series, for example. In real terms, the P cab measured 2,790 mm to the top of its roof, the R cab 3,045 and the T cab 2,850. If the snorkel air stack was fitted, which it generally was unless special equipment was specified, then the height was 270 mm more in all cases. The low-height G cab was actually identical to the P and was mounted exactly the same on the chassis, the height difference being achieved by a cranked front axle and special springs. *(Photos: Clive Burnet and Scania AB)*

Program Scania, certainly as far as the UK was concerned, really kicked off in May 1981 when the company ramped up its activities in the trade journals with a lavish four-page colour advertisement featuring a stunning blue 142 rigid, which also appeared in the first brochure. The accompanying text covered two and a half pages and explained a great deal about the G P R range and aspects of its development. A more concise version of the advert was still running in June.

Also key to the promotional activity was the 'Scania Roadshow'. This tour which got under way on 26 May, featured an array of consecutively registered vehicles from the range, both artics and rigids. It covered twenty-seven dates through May, June and July utilising the premises of noted Scania dealerships such as B & W Motors, Morville Trucks and a selection of Scantruck and Scanlink depots to show off the vehicles and allow interested parties to look them over.

The van trailer, pulled by a R112 fitted with full air kit, presumably carried hospitality and, no doubt, a ready supply of brochures. To help prospective customers become familiar with the new models, Scania applied the truck's designation to the doors in the lower decal stripe, some of which were in just one colour. Note that TNM 809W was not fitted with a sun visor and that TNM 808W was fitted with a roof rack, the latter perhaps to enforce the TIR image of the R142. Driver, enthusiast and author Ashley Coghill caught up with the trucks at Scania's Milton Keynes headquarters towards the end of the tour in July 1981. *(Photos: Ashley Coghill)*

Two splendid R142s and each laying claim to be the first of the type registered in their respective countries of England and Scotland. Although the author cannot validate either claim, they are clearly both early examples and very fine specimens at that. With promotional activity occurring in the three-month lead up to the new registration date of 1 August, it is perhaps unsurprising that W-registered examples were so few and perhaps only restricted to Scania's own ex-demonstration fleet. In fact, there was still LB stock being sold by the dealerships at the time and X-registered 111s and 141s were not uncommon.

W Scholey's handsome example makes a fine sight shrouded in English Channel fog as it waits at Dover in September 1981.

Caught taking a break at Forton Services, John Greig's R142 with its superbly executed livery looked splendid coupled to this tri-axle cattle trailer.

Interestingly, neither of these early units is fitted with a sun visor, an item which became almost de rigueur for 2-series trucks, though the Scholey truck did have one fitted in the secondary role of under-bump air deflector. *(Photos: Ashley Coghill)*

This fine comparison, courtesy of the Irish operator Carna, shows clearly the amazing family resemblance that Scania and Giugiaro managed to achieve in the new cab design, particularly when viewed from head on. Lights, grilles, badges and bumpers all followed a similar pattern and position on the new trucks. Scania even managed to retain a two-wiper system, when many rivals were opting for three, and the central exterior mounted cap for the radiator header tank. While mimicking the old grille with its slats and spacing, the new item was now one-piece and manufactured from GRP (glass-reinforced plastic). It also rose on gas struts to ease level checks to be made for oil and water. *(Photo: Steve Lynch)*

Although there is the effect of perspective to be taken into account here, the medium-height P cab was indeed considerably taller than that of the Volvo F86. The F86 was replaced by the F7, which offered a larger cab and could justifiably have been put in the same class as Scania's previous smaller-cabbed truck, the LB81. However, with the introduction of Scania's new cab, with a common width across G P and R variants, the goal posts were moved giving Scania a truck with F10 performance but a low-profile cab and no interior width restrictions for the driver. *(Photo: Marcus Lester)*

This hard-worked unit in G P R launch livery and decal stripes could well have been an ex-demonstrator and it would appear the operator took the easier option of painting the trailer to match the unit, a wise decision when the truck looked this good. Available as Scania accessories along with the air horns also fitted here, the decal stripes came in a number of colour combinations.

Note the extra diesel tank and the minor damage to the bumper, which has resulted in the loss of the bottom step. *(Photo: Marcus Lester)*

Russell Davies, an experienced Scania operator of many years standing, took on large numbers of early 2-series trucks to work alongside its older LB units and both the 11-litre and 14-litre engines were much in evidence. Despite the increase in power for the V8 to 388 bhp, it would seem that general hauliers were starting to appreciate that the big 14-litre engine was not necessarily a gas-guzzler and that, if driven well, it could return very creditable mpg figures.

At the time Russell Davies still preferred a 4 x 2 set-up and many units ran with the full Scania air kit, a logical addition considering that the company's work was so heavily biased towards container traffic. *(Photo: Marcus Lester)*

Spot the difference? Although the colours and name are different there was no disguising the influence of Russell Davies on the livery of Felgate Transport once it had taken over the much smaller concern.

Felgate provided an R112M unit for *Truck* magazine to test early in 1982. The magazine was some way behind rival *Commercial Motor*, which had tested TNM 810W, one of the ex-roadshow fleet, back in December 1981. The late test and the use of an operator's truck may have been the result of *Truck* breaking the embargo on the G P R information and publishing it early in December 1980 (actually its January 1981 edition). This could have been the test vehicle as the photographs in the magazine, which featured AJN 414X, were taken separately due to poor weather conditions. *(Photo: Adrian Cypher)*

Following what the LB140 had started back in 1969 and the LB141 had built on since 1976, the 142 made the perfect truck for long distance TIR work at the start of the new decade. The 14-litre V8 engine, now designated DS14 06, pumped out 388 bhp and a colossal 1,164 lb/ft of torque, making it the most powerful production truck in Europe. The type was particularly popular with owner-drivers who favoured the truck because the engine worked well within its limits, giving great reliability. Note how the white-painted headlight surrounds altered this truck's appearance.

(Photo: David Wakefield)

Photographed on the Austrian border in May 2000, this early 112 was heading for home in Macedonia via the former Yugoslavia, proving there was still a good deal of life left in it.

By 1980, Scania's reputation for quality and longevity was legend. Since the LB76 arrived in the UK back in 1967 the marque had proved itself in all sorts of operations. However, despite the LB76's prowess, Scania instigated a replacement program in the early 1970s, such was its determination to stay ahead of the competition. That program brought the LB range into existence, which effectively became the unofficial 1-series through the mid-life developments that resulted in the LB81, 111 and 141.

(Photo: Andreas Wolst)

A fresh blue-based livery replaced the former green one and heralded the arrival of 2-series Scanias in the own-account fleet of industrial valve manufacturer, Pegler & Louden.

Glasgow-based driver Jim Low transferred to this smart R142 from an equally smart LB141 that was registered just a little earlier on a W-plate. The LB141 was bought new and put in three years' work hauling valves around the UK before replacement, so presumably the R142 was purchased second-hand?

Jim's twin air horn arrangement and 'Diane' plate also made the transfer to the R142. Note the blue-painted steps. *(Photo: Marcus Lester)*

Of course there were some who felt that the excellent R cab just didn't have enough room and as Scania didn't offer a Globetrotter style high-roof option it was down to individuals and enterprising outside concerns to come up with suitable alterations, generally from fibre-glass. However, this intrepid effort has not only gone up but back as well with a nicely executed extension in the rear side panel. Hopefully the builder also strengthened the cab floor and up-rated the cab tilt ram to handle the extra weight.

(Photo: David Wakefield)

When it was introduced, the 112 could be specified with one of two versions of the 11-litre engine. The DS11 14 produced 280 bhp and 860 lb/ft of torque, making it ideal for long-distance general haulage in the UK, while the DS11 15 produced 305 bhp and 911 lb/ft of torque for those requiring just that little bit more power. Significantly, both engines now ran to a maximum of 2,000 rpm and delivered peak torque at 1,300 rpm. This was a further move down the 'lugger' type engine route that the company had started with the LB111of 1974 in the interests of better fuel economy and prolonged engine life.

Unfortunately, as output badges did not emerge until the introduction of the 3-series trucks, it was never possible to know what tune of engine was beneath the cab of 112s.

Note the tight trailer clearance on the rear wings of this Irish own-account machine. *(Photo: Adrian Cypher)*

As there was just one version of the DS14 available for early 142s, there was no such confusion over the engine output. However, with badges removed there was actually no way of telling a 142 from a 112, apart from the engine note. Some unscrupulous operators used this to their advantage by running overloaded 142s with 112 badges to explain the apparent absence of V8 performance on the hills, a scam that had also previously been applied to the LB141/ LB111.

However, there is no reason to doubt the credentials of this stunning R142 as it sweeps into Dover. Note the cylindrical container mounted beside the battery tray, which is possibly a water carrier. *(Photo: David Wakefield)*

The extension of the modular system to include the same basic cab throughout the range meant that the 112, unlike the old LB111, was not necessarily all about glamour any more. Few would dispute that the outgoing LB111 with its high-profile cab was anything other than a premium truck and just a notch below the LB141 in desirability. However, with the introduction of the 2-series it was now possible to have 112 performance in a more humble package, which was actually well suited to domestic haulage in most countries. With a lower price than an R cab equipped equivalent, it was also attractive for big fleet use, a sector in which Scania had not been particularly strong previously but wished to increase its market share.

This tidy unit of Western Transport, exemplifies the new, less traditional role that Scania hoped to fill with the P112. *(Photo: Marcus Lester)*

Truck manufacturers have always locked on to high-profile operators for good publicity and will generally fall over themselves to get representation in such fleets. These companies need not be big, just the best at what they do and that invariably means being the first to take on new ventures and tap new markets. For Middle East transport there was one true pioneering company, Astran. If ever there was a haulage company that attained international renown, in a ratio far beyond its modest size, it was this bold outfit of adventurers from England.

However, Scania did not have to chase Astran for business, as the company considered that Scania offered the best trucks for the job anyway.

Astran had been plying its trade to the Middle East for over fifteen years by the time the 2-series was launched and had been using Scanias for its operations since 1967. Despite a handful of LB140s, mostly drawbars that arrived in the mid-1970s, the buying policy tended to focus on the 11-litre powered trucks with the LB111 being the most prolific type operated. With the introduction of the 2-series this trend changed. No more 11-litre powered trucks were bought and the R142 in 4 x 2 tractor format became the standard choice. Apart from hired-in trucks, and those of sub-contractors, the only deviation from Scania came in the shape of three Mercedes-Benz S1632s, which were delivered shortly before the first R142s. The German trucks were supplied by Sparshatt's of Kent and they were among the first vehicles to be supplied through its new premises in Sittingbourne, Kent. Despite being kitted out for desert operations, with Hubbard air conditioning and forward-mounted air intakes, the Mercs failed to impress Astran drivers who found the 16-litre V10 engines, although offering more bhp, to be almost 100 lb/ft down in torque compared to their old LB111s.

AOO 67X is seen in contrast with minarets in the Middle East and at the company's West Malling base along with AOO 66X. Note how sun and sand exposure has taken a toll on the badges. *(Photos: Astran Collection & Steve Lynch)*

A stunning line-up of R142s and T112s awaiting delivery, most likely in one of the South American countries which became so important to Scania, especially Brazil, its biggest single market. Scania had a presence in Brazil from as early as 1953 when a third-party company assembled CKD kits shipped from Sweden, but strict local laws brought in to kerb the country's dire financial state required Scania to establish its own manufacturing plant in 1962. A plant in Argentina followed in 1976 with each supplying the other and even Sweden with parts. *(Photo: Scania AB)*

The comparison between Volvo's F10/12 and Scania's 112/142 was inevitable and fuelled much discussion between drivers. Of course, as vehicles constructed within the constraints of legislation to perform the same task, the two were dynamically very similar. Probably the biggest difference was the ride characteristics, and which one was better or preferable was down to the individual driver. Volvo's sophisticated four-point cab suspension was the best in the business and provided a 'magic carpet' ride, but some found it over-insulating, making them feel remote from what was happening at road level, and so preferred the harder feel of the Scania system.

Note that the operator retained the Globetrotter launch livery for this F12 and that the Scania has a rather creased door.

(Photo: Ashley Coghill)

The GRP grille of the 2-series mimicked the wide bar and spacing appearance of the old LB and was in marked contrast to virtually all other manufacturers that had adopted some form of black mesh grille at the time. How an operator chose to paint it could greatly change the appearance of the truck. Some picked out the bars in the livery colour and painted the spaces black, others kept the sides and bars one colour with just the area in front of the radiator black. Here, on this fine example operated by Bon Accord, a large black centre section has almost created the look of a black grille rather like that of an F10. *(Photo: Ashley Coghill)*

This R112M was part of the initial press demonstration fleet and actually graced the cover of *Truck's* embargo-breaking edition. To emphasise the diversity offered by the modular system, the demo fleet was a mixed bag of sometimes unlikely trucks, and DTA 634 was one such vehicle. The bright yellow unit with matching trailer was supposed to represent a European-spec 38-tonner. Mechanically it fitted the bill nicely with the DS11 14 giving 280 bhp and the GR 870 10-speed range type gearbox. However, the day cab and what appears to be the smallest capacity diesel tank, which was usually fitted on the left of the chassis as an addition to a larger tank on the right, were perhaps a curious choice for the intended representation. *(Photo: Scania AB)*

This stunning example of an R142 operated by David C Ball shows how a beautifully presented yet understated livery can work just as well, and often better, than a more complex one.

Ancillaries on the old LB chassis, such as air tanks and batteries, were mounted either side, which, while aesthetically pleasing in their symmetry, did require extra plumbing and made servicing and fault-finding a longer process. On the 2-series all the air tanks and batteries were now positioned together on the left of the chassis in an identical layout for all types. *(Photo: Ashley Coghill)*

The modular components of the H (heavy) chassis and RD830 hub reduction axle from the 2-sries range that formed the basis of this R112 suggest that it was employed on seriously long and arduous TIR routes. Factor in the 6 x 2 format and Trilex wheels and it is almost certain that destinations included the Middle East for this Turkish outfit. The lifting trailing axle was something of a Scania speciality – though Volvo also offered one – and it was a layout that it stood by in preference to a 6 x 4 for most operations other than dedicated heavy haulage. The AS90 trailing axle had a capacity of 7,000 kg. *(Photo: Adrian Cypher)*

Unusually, given the company's name and the R142's abilities, Atkins International operated one such machine on a domestic contract at 32 tons, which would have been odd had it not been for the 'just in time' nature of the job and the heavy penalty for non-delivery. That R142 replaced an earlier LB141 that had previously serviced the same contract.

It was therefore very appropriate for *Truck* magazine, still in Scania's bad books at the time, to borrow the truck, SVO 251X, for a comparison test of 350 bhp-plus tractors at 32 tons. The envisaged three-way test was to pitch the Scania against an F12 and Bedford's E370-powered TM4400, the three 350 bhp-plus trucks then available in the UK without being subject to special order, but Volvo pulled out at the eleventh hour leaving the Scania to thrash it out with the big Bedford alone. Both trucks ran the test without any air management devices and flat trailers loaded with test weights. The two trucks actually came out even on the overall earning factor as the Scania's better speed and lower mpg were offset by the Bedford's lighter weight, which gave an increased payload. The fact that two 350 bhp machines could achieve average fuel figures in the region of 7.5 mpg was testament to the work that both Scania and Cummins had put in to make their respective 14-litre engines considerably more economical than their predecessors. The test deemed them both viable for UK 32-ton operation.

(Photo: Marcus Lester)

The air management kit developed by Scania could do much to improve the mpg figure of any truck in the 2-series range that was destined to work with tall trailers. The final design of the air deflector and side panel system, as seen here, was the result of extensive wind tunnel testing on half-scale models. Test results showed a drop of 21 per cent in resistance for a tractor unit with high trailer fitted with just the roof deflector and 30 per cent when also fitted with the side deflectors. The system gave its best results at motorway speeds when air resistance would ultimately be greater than rolling resistance. *(Photo: Marcus Lester)*

Of course for some operators, such as Tony Morgan, there were no benefits to be had from fitting wind-cheating add-ons. For plant haulage firms with some of the most air turbulent loads imaginable, Scania's air management system would have proved a costly encumbrance.

However, even those operators benefited from the wind tunnel testing which identified the optimum cab corner radii and windscreen rake to make the cab alone as slippery through the air as possible.

Tony Morgan also ran the consecutively registered R142, MWO 298X, along with the Volvo and Leyland Marathons hiding behind here. The R142s were near identical, but MWO 298X did not have its grille picked out in red. (Photo: Marcus Lester)

The cab designation system adopted for the 2-series was both simple and logical. All variants started with the letter C followed by the class G, P, R or T, then 13 or 19 for day cab and sleeper respectively. For example, here we have a CP 19-equipped 112 of Spalding Haulage and a CR 19 cabbed 142 operated by Baybutt.

Scania's cab production facility in Oskarshamn, 320 km south of the main production facility at Södertälje, started building the new 2-series cab following the summer shutdown in 1980, initially for the T-series trucks. The cab was made up of some 3,000 components and the finished items, trimmed and ready to meet the chassis, were transported north eight at a time on purpose-built trucks that ran virtually around the clock to supply Södertälje production.

At the time, Oskarshamn was second only in size to Södertälje and its 1,600-plus workforce also produced CKD cab kits for export to a number of Scania's overseas facilities. *(Photos: Marcus Lester and Ashley Coghill)*

John C Spencer's haulage business evolved through his farming activities. In the early 1970s he ran a four-wheeler Ford, with beaver tail bodywork, to move his own crawler and other equipment. This soon attracted customers requiring a similar service and led to the purchase of a Ford artic unit. An offer of running abroad for a friend resulted in a chrome grille F88 240 replacing the Ford. Continental work went well and an introduction to Leggett European saw a second F88 join the first, both running out of Leggett's Chingford depot. Work for Yorkshire Imperial Plastics also brought long-distance UK work, with Scotland a common destination. However, plant movement was just as important and trucks capable of performing the dual role were always favoured. The company's first Scania was a second-hand LB141 purchased from Telford Motors, Cardiff. John had spotted the advertisement for the truck but told the guy on the phone, who turned out to be Bob Penrose, that unfortunately he could not get to view it in office hours for a few days. Bob said he would be happy to hang around for John that day and the sale was actually made at 9 pm that evening following a short test drive. Not only did the LB141 impress, but so did Bob and an enduring friendship was the result.

These two views of the subsequent R142, XFD 552X, performing its most typical role with semi-low loader and low loader trailers, shows the neat chassis installations of the 2-series trucks, particularly in a 4 x 2 format. It also illustrates the smart Spencer livery to great effect. *(Photos: Marcus Lester)*

It is slightly ironic, in the author's opinion, that Sweden, producer of the finest heavy trucks in Europe, operated an efficient state railway system that was so highly geared to moving freight that it limited the number of heavy trucks required for domestic haulage. Svelast was the railway's road transport division and while it operated huge numbers of trucks, many were in the lower weight categories. Volvo, Scania and Mercedes-Benz all figured largely in the fleet. Scania's 2-series, like the LB range before, was well regarded, especially the P82 which was operated in a number of rigid formats. The breakdown and trans-shipping of goods from the railway hubs meant that short hauls were the norm so the vast majority of Svelast trucks, including many of the artic units, were only fitted with day cabs. This R112 was obviously one of the trucks expected to run much greater distances, equipped as it was with the CR 19 sleeper cab, roof rack and ladder.

Note the generous engine access afforded by the 60-degree tilt angle of the cab. *(Photo: Scania AB)*

Astran were not the only UK firm to put early examples of the R142 on Middle East work. Funstons, a small and plucky family firm from Hertfordshire, had been running to the Middle East for six years by 1981 when they purchased this unit and another with 6 x 2 layout, which mainly hauled to Spain. XKX 518X went to long-serving driver, Noel Walker, and he was mightily happy with his new charge. The truck was fitted with the Scania roof rack which Noel later used to mount a water tank with washer bottle pump to provide a shower facility. Funstons generally ran with these distinct road/rail tilts, but the company also had a standard twin-axle tilt in its colours but with 'Pif Paf' written in large letters down the sides in both English and Arabic. This was used for one of the company's regular contracts, which involved hauling fly spray of that name, from Berkhamsted to Saudi Arabia.

The truck is seen parked up on the H4 in Jordan and tipping at a factory complex in Riyadh where Noel always took the opportunity to wash the truck down.

Note how Funstons adapted the Volvo stripe decal to become part of its standard livery. *(Photos: Noel Walker)*

By 1980 Scania was producing 30,000 engines a year from the 8-, 11- and 14-litre ranges, but not all went into trucks and buses with plant, generators and marine applications all accounting for a large proportion of that figure. However, the numbers going into service, whatever the role, were proving invaluable for providing in-field statistics to back up Scania's own research and development programs for engines. Scania had been pushing the low-revving concept to save fuel since 1975 and prior to the launch of the 2-series it ran a trial with, coincidentally, 112 drivers that were monitored over 350 long-distance routes. Its findings were remarkable and showed a 40 per cent variation in fuel economy through driver technique.

Although obviously a consideration, the tight schedules of Promotor International's core exhibition/tour work meant that fuel economy definitely came second to speed and reliability. *(Photo: Steve Lynch)*

This R142 drawbar combination constructed on the H chassis was fairly typical of the type that was popular throughout Europe when the 2-series was introduced. However, maximum-weight drawbars were a rare choice for UK operators, where the artic combination still ruled the roost. As a result, Scania did not offer the 142 drawbar chassis with right-hand drive. Dealers were less than enthusiastic about any enquiries for such vehicles as they feared being lumbered with a truck that would be tricky to sell if the original deal fell through. However, Germany was a good market for drawbars and this fine example operating in the famed wine-making region of the Mosel Valley makes a handsome combination with its three-axle trailer. *(Photo: Scania AB)*

A different continent, South America, and a different approach to grape production, but the locally built Scania product was much the same here as it was for the rest of the world. An interesting feature of many South American produced trucks in the 2-series range was the subtle 'S' badge, which was applied to the grille opposite the model designation. It can only be assumed that this stood for 'super', the word Scania originally attached to a vehicle fitted with the turbocharged version of an engine – for example, the DS11 rather than the normally aspirated D11. Scania first applied the 'super' script to a grille on the L75, its first turbocharged truck, and its derivatives in 1958.

(Photo: Scania AB)

H C Wilson ran two R112s on its abnormal load work, much of which involved the movement of farm machinery in and out of the UK. At the time the two new Scanias worked alongside Wilson's old LB141 – a truck the company still owns at the time of writing – and a mix of other types from Leyland, Foden and DAF. Following on in Wilson tradition the truck carried a 'Harvester' prefixed name, in this case, 'Duke', which is just visible on the sun visor.

By 1989 the truck had moved from Suffolk to Kent and was operated as a second unit by owner-driver, Steve Packer. The R112 was given a new livery and handed to a young driver, Mark Robinson. Mark, still just twenty-one, fresh from passing his test and only on his second artic following a 1979 F10, could not believe his luck at being charged with the powerful Scania.

H C Wilson also applied the name 'Harvester Duke' to E182 GBJ, a much later R142.

Note that the original roof beacons survived the chassis and cab re-paint that came with the change of ownership. *(Photos: David Wakefield and Mark Robinson)*

Toni Huber, a Swiss owner-driver, put this beautifully presented early R142 to work exclusively for Hangartner. The truck featured a fairly typical continental spec with some Swiss market additions such as the Trilex wheels. Chassis modifications, involving the repositioning of some of the air tanks and the valves that were usually mounted next to the battery tray, allowed for a larger auxiliary diesel tank to be mounted on the left of the chassis within the 3.4-metre wheelbase.

As the 142 did not conform to Switzerland's regulations, which limited trucks to a maximum width of 2,300 mm, its use inside the country was restricted, but in common with many Hangartner trucks, both own-account vehicles and those of sub-contractors, it was operated in a truly international way.

The truck is pictured at rest when brand new with a Hangartner van trailer and slightly later with one of the company's more familiar tilts in tow as it drops into Dover. By this time it has gained air horns, running lights and a degree of personalisation and, indeed, another driver, Rico, who was hired by Toni.

Note the sand planks attached to the cab ladder, items as useful for negotiating snow as they were for gaining traction on sand.

(Photos: Paul Willis and David Wakefield)

This late LB111 and early R112 operated by ABLE from its Leighton Buzzard depot, show clearly the different thinking applied to doors between the old and the new range, one of the major design differences between the two. The exposed step arrangement of the G P R forward control trucks made a bold statement and did much to enhance the aggressive look of the new trucks. Some early press comments expressed a degree of surprise at a move away from the covered steps of the old LB range, feeling that this made them vulnerable to fouling and freezing and thus slippery and dangerous. In practice, however, these fears were unfounded as the open grid pattern was self-draining and, to a large extent, self-cleaning due to its exposure to the elements. Given the extensive wind tunnel testing that Scania carried out, it is fair to assume that the open arrangement did not come with an unacceptable effect on drag, either. Also, the open design simplified the engineering differences that were required to manufacture doors for the different height cabs of the modular system. *(Photo: Ashley Coghill)*

By the end of May 1982, Scania had taken third place in the all-important 28-tonne and over tractor unit sector in the UK, second only to Volvo and DAF. This position, although initially bolstered by operators sweeping up the last of the LBs, reflected well on the new 2-series trucks and marked something of a sea change for Scania in the UK. Interestingly, as far as the UK was concerned, the 112 powered by the DS11 14 was the most popular followed by the slightly more powerful DS11 15 version of the same truck and then the 142. Surprisingly, the 82, which was capable of UK general haulage, albeit in slightly less glamorous fashion, came last on the list.

For an own-account operator like ASL Airflow, running at a maximum of 32 tons and probably a good deal less given the high-cube nature of its plastic products for house and garden, the 280 bhp of the DS11 14 would have been ample, even for cross-channel ventures as undertaken by this unit returning through Dover in the mid 1980s.

Curries, on the other hand, would almost certainly have opted for the higher output of 305 bhp as offered by the DS11 15, which also gave a useful 51 lb/ft increase in torque over the 860 of the DS11 14.

Note the after-market wind deflector fitted to the ASL truck and the minor livery differences of the nearly new Curries pair pictured at rest in France.

(Photos: David Wakefield and Ashley Coghill)

45

By the summer of 1981, Astran was enjoying a trading boom with an increase in traffic to Iraq, Qatar and UAE markets that had seen business up by 50 per cent. A £300,000 investment in equipment saw ten new trailers purchased and the company's last batch of own-account tractor units, in the form of three R142s, before a policy change saw a complete switch to sub-contractors for traction. The consecutively registered Scanias, EKO 948, 949 and 950Y closely followed the purchase of two more Mercedes-Benz units and brought the number of R142s operated up to seven. The Mercedes-Benz units were the new 1633 model, which, being fitted with the large G-cab and more powerful V8 engines, were far more acceptable to Astran drivers than the unloved 1632s purchased earlier. Despite Mercedes gaining a late toehold in the fleet, it was somehow appropriate for a company that had forged such strong links with Scania to mark its final truck purchase with the three R142s.

Note Astran's LB81 shunter in the background. This truck, which was used to ferry trailers to and from the docks, was new in 1981 and replaced an ageing F86 in this vital role.

[Photos: Steve Lynch]

Eurotrux was based in the wonderfully named village of Pucklechurch just to the north-east of Bristol and was mostly engaged in the concert tour/exhibition sector. As such, it required fast, reliable and comfortable trucks to maintain schedules and, quite literally, ensure that the show went on. 2-series Scanias started arriving soon after the G R P launch to work alongside and eventually replace older LB models. The company also became something of a specialist in taking loads to Russia and at one time its vehicles accounted for nearly 40 per cent of UK trucks bound for the Iron Curtain and beyond.

This R112 is pictured at the Meadowbank stadium in Edinburgh while engaged on the Prince tour of 1999. *(Photo: John W Henderson)*

For many Eastern Block drivers trucking was a truly unglamorous affair. In Yugoslavia, for example, roads were poor and dangerous, and the crude domestic offerings from TAM and FAP were hopelessly underpowered compared to trucks from western manufacturers. However, the lucky few who got to drive internationally were thankfully equipped with the appropriate machinery for the task, such as this fine R112H. Built on the heavy H chassis, this unit was more than capable of absorbing the punishment of Yugoslavian roads, even the notorious Autoput, the alleged truck highway through the country, which for much of its length was only a single lane.

Note the missing diesel tank, though the brackets and straps remain. *(Photo: David Wakefield)*

The author must confess to being somewhat confused by this image of an early R112H, which to all appearances would seem to be storming an Alpine pass. While a publicity shot of an un-registered truck and with some detail obscured by the dazzling effect of the headlights, it is clear to see an 'S' badge, as fitted to 2-series trucks produced in Brazil at the bottom of the grille. The truck also has Trilex wheels, an unusual under-bumper bar and what appears to be a 1-series (LB) diesel tank. Graffiti on the tunnel opening clearly mentions Chueca, a town near Madrid, Spain and a date near the end of 1981, making the chances of this being a 'bitsa' pre-production prototype very unlikely. Answers on a postcard please! *(Photo: Scania AB)*

Despite the reluctance of UK dealers to take orders for drawbars, there was nonetheless a small market, usually among the more specialist hauliers such as Peter Gilder for whom, despite also running artic combinations, the operational benefits of a rigid truck and trailer were often beneficial. Gilder was a great fan of Scania and had this capable truck created from a stretched tractor unit to fulfil his requirements. The biggest clue to his conversion is the tractor unit diesel tank which is fitted, rather than the longer, shallower item fitted to factory-built rigid chassis. *(Photo: David Wakefield)*

Scania, like Volvo, manufactured its own gearboxes and, like Volvo, had long championed full synchromesh over crash-type units for the ease of driving. The gearboxes of the 2-series range were further developments of previous designs and had, indeed, been subject to constant improvements since their introduction on the L75 some twenty years previously. As well as making the gearboxes more robust and reliable, Scania also moved the gear stick position in the cab, which did away with the long, vague lever of the old LBs, and gave the 2-series trucks a much more ergonomic item with a shorter throw and more precision.

Aston Clinton Haulage also ran good numbers of older LBs in its smart fleet. *(Photo: David Wakefield)*

Scania and Volvo can directly claim the credit for the major shift towards synchromesh gearboxes for heavy trucks. Both companies, as far as Europe was concerned, came to the fore in the late 1960s and their respective market share grew dramatically through the following decade. In the same period, gearbox manufacturer ZF recorded an increase of nearly 30 per cent in demand for its synchromesh boxes as other truck manufacturers, desperate to match the appeal of the Swedish trucks, started to fit the type in ever increasing numbers.

Note the grille modifications to this R142, which, combined with the stripes, give a definite US flavour, and the overspray on the front and rearmost wheels, possibly as a result of chassis work in the form of a tag axle conversion. *(Photo: David Wakefield)*

Inter City Trucks ran a largely Volvo fleet when the 2-series was launched. Scania were keen to get representation in the Kent firm and provided this R142M for an extended demonstration period, which ran to nearly two months. Driver John Bartholomew was very impressed with the power of the big V8 engine and argued the case for Scania purchases to be made. However, he would have to wait and ultimately settle for an R112.

Although the company stopped running its own trucks in the early 2010s, Inter City is still in business at the time of writing using sub-contractors for traction. *(Photo: Paul Willis)*

Scania were keen to promote the British content of the new 2-series and claimed to be providing around 2,500 jobs via the regular orders that it placed with 250 UK companies for components used on the range. In addition, Scania also claimed that the distribution of its vehicles employed another 700. These figures were important for Scania and perhaps eased the conscience of operators that were starting to think of moving away from domestically produced trucks.

Swains made its move over to Scania in the late 1960s when it started operating LB110s alongside its traditional fleet of ERFs and Seddons and soon built a reputation as an international haulier of note with the Swedish machines frequenting the far-flung corners of Europe. *(Photo: Paul Willis)*

Although in considerably better shape than the F88 beside it, this early R142 is starting to show the signs of age. The 2-series cab generally fared pretty well with regard to rust and was definitely a marked improvement over the old LB design. Door bottoms, as here, were prone to rust if chips caused by keys, rings or contact with walls and loading bays were not addressed, though typically this would generally only affect the driver's door, through use. The cab doors originally opened to 92 degrees, but this was quickly reduced to 87 degrees, as it required a good long reach to shut them from the seats – a problem for shorter drivers who actually ran the risk of falling out.

Windscreen surrounds would also rust eventually, but not until well into the truck's useful life.

This R142, used for the delivery of fruit from Kent to the London markets, was a lot of truck for the job and operated under the GLC exemption notice of the time allowing access through the capital's night ban. *(Photo: Paul Willis)*

ROBA UK, part of the Bowater Freight Group, had run V8 Scanias since the original LB140, when it operated as W & M Wood, and was highly impressed with the performance of the DS14 in each of its previous versions. Naturally, R142s followed the LB141s that had replaced the LB140s and the new trucks were soon recording an impressive 8.0 mpg on the company's continental work. This was even better than the figures that *Truck* magazine had managed to coax from an R142 in its Eurotest of 1981. The testers had been highly impressed with the average of 6.54 mpg which had placed the big Scania 4th on the table, five places above the LB141 tested in 1979.

ROBA UK's R142s tended to run without roof deflectors as early units fitted with the device suffered from stress cracking around the mounting holes on the roof, making the mpg figures even more impressive.

Note how close the registration is to that of the Payne Farms' unit above.

(Photo: Paul Willis)

A valuable aid in the design and development of the 2-series was Scania's STRASS computer program. The Scania Transport Simulation System was able to give accurate results for virtual journeys by virtual trucks of varying spec and saved huge amounts of time in the development stages. Interestingly, the system could be used to simulate trucks running together, as could often be the case for an operator in real life. In a simulated comparison of one DS14-powered truck with one DS11-powered one, the findings were that the smaller-engined vehicle would use more fuel in trying to maintain pace with the larger one. While not wholly surprising, the beauty of the system was that it could break down the result and actually list the number of extra gear changes required by the DS11-powered truck. It even gave the DS11s greater number of engine revolutions which, for a journey on Sweden's E4, turned out to be 150 more per kilometre than for the DS14-powered machine.

It was not unusual for an operator to run examples of both 11- and 14-litre Scanias, Martintrux of Tilbury being one. This was the first 2-series bought by the company. *(Photo: Ashley Coghill)*

As the saying goes, 'you pays your money and you takes your choice'. Although some companies resolutely supported one Swedish manufacturer rather than the other, a very great number found that both had different merits and were happy to include both in their fleets, especially any company undertaking continental work. There was certainly no denying the driver appeal of Volvo or Scania and most drivers would have been more than happy with either.

As part of its low-speed program, Volvo actually de-rated its non-intercooled F12 in 1981, effectively bringing it in line with the more powerful version of the 112 in terms of bhp. However, the TD120G engine of the F12 possessed higher torque than the DS11 15 of the 112 and its excellent sixteen-speed gearbox allowed it to come close to the 142 in performance. *Truck* magazine pitted a TD120G-powered F12 against the R142 that it ran in its Eurotest of 1981. The Volvo was less than 1 mph slower and marginally better on fuel, but the Scania just beat it on productivity due to its slightly lower weight. *(Photo: Ashley Coghill)*

This interesting comparison of a TIR R142 and more humble 112 with the P cab, shows how Scania's modular cab system utilised the same front wheel arch assembly for the different-height cabs. The raised mouldings visible on the front of the wheel arch could be used in different combinations to mount the steps, depending on the cab variant. The steps themselves were extremely wide and positioned like a ladder with each step slightly further in than the one below, which made getting in and out an easy and safe process whatever height the cab. The G cab, although actually the same as the P cab – just lower through changes to the chassis – had only two steps. The bottom one was joined to both the bumper and the wheel arch and was unique to the type (see page 17).

Note the pleasing proportions of the P112 and the older LB111 in the background.

(Photos: David Wakefield and Marcus Lester)

Dennis Oates started his company in 1951 with an old Commer that fortunately came with an O-licence. Specialising in the movement of produce and flowers out of Cornwall to the rest of the country allowed for steady growth, though the firm always retained the family feel. British trucks gave way to Volvos and the Gothenburg machines became the mainstay of the small fleet until the early 1980s. Problems with rust on his F10s led Dennis to look at other makes and it was not long before the first Scania arrived in the shape of an LB141 4 x 2 tractor. The truck was bought second-hand and direct from owners Brain Haulage. It was one of number waiting to go into service with the Essex haulier and was essentially new with no more than delivery miles on the clock. Dennis was immediately impressed and it was not long before an order was placed with Unit Commercials Ltd of Salisbury for a brand-new R142 and R112. The consecutively registered, SAF 101Y and SAF 102Y left little change from £70,000.

The beautiful Oates livery of maroon and grey always looks superb, but was especially good when applied to the handsome lines of two new R cabs.

Dennis was soon seeing 9 mpg from the new Scanias. Driver acceptance was very high, some even rating the R112 over the older but more powerful LB141, probably because of the more comfortable cab and ride.

(Photos: Marcus Lester)

The entire 2-series range was equipped with a power-assisted, recirculating ball steering system by the German manufacturer ZF which combined with the generous geometry of the front wheels to provide an excellent lock. The turning circle was correspondingly very tight at just 11.96 m for a 4 x 2 tractor with a 3.4 m wheelbase. This was virtually class-leading for premium tractors; only DAF managed a tighter turning circle of 11.90 m with an equivalent product, albeit with a marginally longer wheelbase of 3.5 m. This made the big Scanias very manoeuvrable, which endeared them to drivers. Steering input was made via a neat, two-spoke wheel of 500 mm diameter, which was adjustable for rake and height and required 5.9 turns from lock to lock. The wheel's spokes were angled back towards the driver allowing an unobstructed view of the instruments.

The immaculate trucks of Walsam Transport and OTA International Transport were virtually indistinguishable from one another. Operated by brothers Pip and Colin Duck respectively, the 'Duck Squadron' of Frome was pretty much one and the same.

Note the '142' outlined on the grille with marker lights. *(Photos: Marcus Lester)*

It did not matter if the work was domestic, as undertaken by this humble 112 of BRS fitted with a P cab or continental long hauls like those made by this Irish-registered R142 TIR express, good back-up from the manufacturer was of paramount importance to any operator. Despite its great reliability record, Scania took back-up very seriously and knew it was a vital part of clinching sales. 'Scania Lifeline' provided UK 2-series customers with a 24-hour emergency service that would despatch help via a free-phone number for eventualities such as breakdown, punctures or broken windscreens. International drivers could count on the support of over 600 service points stretching through Europe to the Middle East. Operators could also manage their costs by tailoring an individual service and repair contract to look after vehicles. In addition, an emergency credit card was available under the 'DKV-Scania EuropaService' scheme, which would cover most emergency repairs.

(Photos: Marcus Lester and David Wakefield)

It was building trucks to work in Sweden's home market that made Scanias so tough. Apart from heavy haulage special types, this 24-metre combination running at the 51.4-tonne limit was very common for maximum weight work. Because of the economy of scale and Scania's modular system, home-market specials were largely unfeasible, which resulted in all markets benefiting from the strength of components needed to perform these roles. The downside for some operators was the higher tare weights of unloaded trucks, but if this was offset over the much longer and trouble-free service life that a Scania would give, the difference became irrelevant.

Note the additional corner deflectors fitted to this hard-worked R142H. *(Photo: Adrian Cypher)*

To prove a point on the longevity afforded to the 2-series by its Swedish roots, this remarkably well-preserved Italian example was spotted working in Trieste in 2012 when at least 24 years old and possibly anything up to 31 years of age. How many of Scania's lighter-weight rivals could offer the same incredible length of service? In addition to the undoubted durability of the chassis, the lazy unstressed nature of the big V8 would also have had a significant effect. Scania had a ready market in Italy for the 2-series. Italscandia, its concessionaire in the country since 1974, held a market share second only to that of IVECO (FIAT). *(Photo: Andreas Wolst)*

Since the demise in the early 1960s of that most British of truck formats, the eight-legger with drawbar trailer, as a premium truck for moving maximum weight loads, the UK had favoured the 4 x 2 tractor as the optimum tool for the job of moving 32 tons on a two-plus-two four-axle combination. In 1983, with the imminent arrival of new legislation allowing 38 tonnes on five axles, the 4 x 2's position at the top was looking to be in question. While truck manufacturers wrestled with the concept and busied themselves testing various types of axle combinations, there was also a wealth of operational unknowns that could affect consumer choice and this left the manufacturers with a problem. Heavy investment in one solution, such as a 6 x 2 twin-steer layout, could prove catastrophic if operators decided to go for three-axle trailers instead. While some manufacturers rushed to provide such a solution, Scania decided to wait it out and stick to what it knew by continuing with its tried and tested 6 x 2 trailing axle layouts, which had served markets with higher weight limits than the UK for years and required no new tooling or chassis changes.

After 1 May 1983, although easily capable of the new weights, the 4 x 2 layout of this wonderful R112 would only have allowed it to operate with a three-axle trailer if the operator wanted to take advantage of the additional weight.

(Photo: Steve Lynch)

While Ferrymasters certainly ran a big fleet with hundreds of trucks, that figure was dwarfed by its trailer operation, which numbered an astonishing three thousand examples in 1983. The ratio of trailers to trucks was high because at any one time a large number would be left unattended while making ferry crossings or loading/unloading at customer locations. It is no surprise, then, that the company thought it more economic to accommodate the change in weight limits by modernising its tractor fleet rather than its trailers.

With a plan to replace around 200 trucks with 6 x 2s by the late summer of 1983, Ferrymasters' business was to be hotly contested by the manufacturers. Unladen weight, over power, was of paramount importance to the deal. Scania was already well represented and highly regarded in the existing fleet with numerous 4 x 2 LB81 and LB82 units operated. With some hasty changes to an available chassis, mainly involving a shortened wheelbase, an initial order for 40 of this 6 x 2 configuration was won.

Note the cylindrical aluminium diesel tank, which was part of the weight-saving method. This item was UK-sourced and thought to have been fitted at Scania's Milton Keynes headquarters. The item also found its way onto Ferrymasters' P112 4 x 2s units.

(Photos: Marcus Lester)

INTERCOOLER

– Lowering temperatures, raising pulses

By the time Scania had introduced its 2-series trucks, intercooling or chargecooling, as the practice was known, had become widespread with most of Scania's key competitors offering one or more engines in their line-ups that were so equipped. In many cases, in terms of outright power, this generally brought the competition up to a similar output as Scania whose engines – particularly the DS14 – were always among the most powerful available. For this reason, Scania had not considered it necessary to introduce the technique of cooling the induction air for its truck engines when it launched the 2-series.

However, with the power gap shrinking rapidly and with a greater understanding of the additional benefits of reduced thermal loadings that intercooling would bring, Scania had a change of policy. In 1981, following a development period, it put 100 prototype units to work with selected operators.

Scania already had a good deal of experience and knowledge of intercooling as it had been applying the method to its marinised DS11 and DS14 for many years. Since autumn 1981 it had offered an intercooled version of the 8-litre engine for transport applications in some countries. In both these cases, however, an air-to-water system was used, whereby diverted engine coolant was passed through a combined heat exchanger/inlet manifold mounted on the left-hand side of the engine. In most respects this system was similar to that used by pure engine builders, such as Cummins. It did not affect anything beyond the engine, was cheap and used up little space, the latter point being especially useful under the lower P cab of the 82.

As the 112 and 142 carried the status of premium trucks and performed the most arduous of tasks, Scania decided to opt for the more technically challenging and expensive method of using air-to-air intercooling for the DS11 and DS14 engines.

The main benefit of this method was a temperature reduction to the air for the cylinders of around 100 degrees as opposed to around 60 degrees for the air-to-water system. The cooler, denser air allowed more fuel to be burnt and increased power accordingly. The heat exchanger was a light alloy radiator that was mounted ahead of the truck's main radiator. This required a minor alteration to the front grille to accommodate it and this changed the profile of the intercooled cabs making them instantly discernible from the standard trucks. The mounting position at the front of the engine meant that the air-to-air system could not initially be applied to 112s fitted with the P cab, so the DS11 14 at 280 bhp became the standard engine for that model, though the 305 bhp DS11 15 could be specified as an option.

As the DSI designation was already being used to identify the marine versions of the 11- and 12-litre engines, the new intercooled ones were to become the DSC11 01 and DSC14 01, the C standing for chargecooling, another popular term for the same process.

The new engines became available early in 1983 and even before confirmation of higher weights for the UK, Scania decided to offer the DSC14 01 to British operators.

Scania displays its engines at the BAUMA exhibition in Munich, Germany. The show was the largest of its kind in Europe and catered for the vehicle and machinery side of the construction industry. Scania found a ready market for its engines in this sector – Kockums using the 8-litre engine for its larger dumpers – and always courted sales for engines as well as trucks at the show. On display here is the marine version of the 14-litre V8, the DSI14, and a DS11-powered standby generator set. Inset is another view of a DSI14. These massive engines for marine use featured intercooling, exhaust cooling and twin turbo installations to provide 750 hp. The 11-litre engine was also popular in the marine sector, one Thames river ferry, Silver Sturgeon, being powered by four DSI11s.

Note the LiAZ tractor unit in the background. Evolved from the truck production of Skoda, the Czech-built LiAZ was the most competent of all the trucks produced behind the Iron Curtain. Not only was there a passing visual resemblance to a DAF, it was also powered by a sub twelve-litre, straight-six engine like the Dutch machine. Output was in the region of 340-350 bhp. (Photos: Scania AB)

Intercooler 001 and presumably 002! This superb photograph shows the new cab profile that accompanied the introduction of the intercooled versions of the 11- and 14-litre engines. Although the heat exchanger radiator only required an additional 100 mm or so of clearance, the new profile, as illustrated by the left-hand truck here, was quite pronounced and changed the appearance of the R cab – softening it somewhat in the author's opinion. The new grille assembly was actually manufactured by the Finnish truck manufacturer Sisu. Badging for the new models was restricted to the subtle 'Intercooler' at the bottom right of the grille, the door decal seen here only being part of the awareness campaign that accompanied the launch. *(Photo: Scania AB)*

The two new engines in all their glory. The DSC11 01 produced 333 bhp at 200 rpm, an increase of 28 bhp over the DS11 15, the next most powerful engine for the 112. Torque was up to 1,025 lb/ft, which represented a useful 114 lb/ft extra, and this new maximum was now produced at 1,250 rpm, which was 50 rpm lower than maximum torque produced in the DS11 15. With reduced thermal loadings, especially throughout the top of the engine, and only a modest 5 per cent increase in internal pressures, Scania was confident that the new engine would maintain the 11-litre's renowned reliability.

With the 14-litre engine, the power increase of 32 bhp gave the DSC14 01 a prodigious 420 bhp, which was produced at 100 rpm less than the 388 bhp of the non-intercooled DS14 06. Torque was now a massive 1,272 lb/ft and this was produced at 1,250 rpm.

These front three-quarter views show the neat alloy radiator that served as the heat exchanger and the exquisite trunking and piping, particularly in the case of the DSC14 01, a true example of the engineer's art in practice. *(Photos: Scania AB)*

In addition to Scania's superb test and research facilities, it could, of course, also make great use of the country's natural habitat, which could provide trying conditions such as this. When coupled to Sweden's generous weight limit of almost 52 tonnes, this provided the perfect environment to develop an engine like the DSC14 01.

This is possibly one of the prototypes that were undergoing field trials with selected operators during 1981, although it is maybe unlikely that the DSC14's presence would have been so boldly advertised if that was the case. Trusted operators were closely involved in the testing of 100 such prototypes and their feedback was vital in the development.

Note the extra circular spotlights fitted to this example and the LB-series truck bringing up the rear. *(Photo: Scania AB)*

The public's first sight of the intercooled engines and trucks came at the Brussels Motor Show in December 1982. On display were cut-away examples of the 8-, 11- and 14-litre engines. An Intercooled R112 and R142 were also shown and these were marked out by a stunning metallic blue paint job in place of the normal white with decal stripes of the other trucks on the stand.

DAF, which obviously got wind of Scania's intended display, occupied the stand opposite and put windscreen stickers on its trucks stating that it had been fitting intercoolers for ten years. This was true enough and the Dutch company was the first European manufacturer to adopt it for production trucks. However, Scania's sales team was quick to point out that it had been intercooling its marine engines for twenty years. *(Photo: Scania AB)*

The press got to try the new intercooled trucks late in 1982. Scania provided an example of each engine fitted to a 6 x 2 drawbar truck with three-axle trailer to the Swedish maximum length of 24 metres and loaded to 52 tonnes. Both the UK's leading magazines attended and were equally impressed during the 150-mile round trip between Scania's main plant and its cab production facility, although the route was an easy one with only modest gradients. The findings were largely predictable in that the big V8 of the 142 made for an effortless cruiser that worked well within its economical green band while making excellent time, and that the 11-litre engine of the 112 required more gear changes to keep pace.

Note the huge spotlights, which are presumably mounted in front of the bumper rather than in it, and the lightweight alloy wheels, surely a curious choice for this line of work. *(Photo: Scania AB)*

The increase in power for the intercooled 112 was possibly more significant than the increase in power for the 142. Although the 420 bhp of the V8 made it easily the most powerful production truck in Europe, the boost for the 112 brought it over the 'magical' 330 bhp mark, which gave Scania representation in a hotly contested and growing sector. The competition here included DAF's recent and excellent 3300, which was also produced specifically to take advantage of the growing trend in this category.

Note the long wheelbase of this fine example.

(Photo: David Wakefield)

The 2-series trucks had proved enormously popular in the UK since the range was launched in 1981. In its first year of sales, Scania sold 919 trucks in the UK, with G P R tractor units outselling domestic brands such as Leyland and ERF. Even Seddon Atkinson, which had often topped the 28-ton-plus tractor market with its 400 – like the one in the background here – and which now fielded its excellent 401 replacement, was overtaken. The timely introduction of the intercooled 112 early in 1983 and this new 6 x 2 chassis ensured that Scania would be ready for the UK's new 38-tonne limit and that sales would not be affected.

(Photo: Marcus Lester)

While the UK seemed ready to embrace the intercooled 112 in anticipation of higher weights, much of Europe was already there. Belgium already allowed a 38-tonne maximum and operators such as this one – with no domestic truck manufacturer besides the highly specialised MOL – were quick to try the new Scania.

The proud driver of this fine example seems keen to place extra emphasis on the presence of the intercooler under the cab.

Note that this unit is built on the H chassis, which was rather unusual for an 11-litre powered 4 x 2.

(Photo: Adrian Cypher)

Toni Huber makes a steady approach to a typical Middle East obstacle in his impressive R142. Well not quite, as this was actually the site entrance to the new Chase Manhattan Bank building in Bournemouth. Hangartner handled much of the international delivery of products for Schmidlin Glass of Aesch, Switzerland. The highly specialised glass was in great demand for use in high-profile buildings at the time. One Hangartner contract involved the movement of bombproof sections of glass for the new MI6 building on the South Bank with a 24-tonne load comprising just six massive pieces.

Toni Huber bought this smart intercooled version after his original R142 (see page 43) was rolled and written off in Luneville, France by a hired driver. The registration is the same as the Swiss system allocates it to the driver for life.

The impressive step-frame trailer featured air suspension and a steering axle at the rear, making manoeuvres such as this a little easier. *(Photo: Paul Willis)*

Despite a generally patriotic stance, most Spanish operators sending trucks out of the country on TIR work did not opt for the domestic products of Pegaso. While straight-forward mechanically and known for a certain agricultural robustness, service back-up in Europe for the Spanish-made truck was poor in comparison to most other European manufacturers. Scania was particularly well served in this respect with extensive service and repair facilities throughout the continent.

Another factor was Pegaso's 12-litre engine which, although capable of producing a healthy 352 bhp, was nowhere near as powerful as the DSC14 01. This was an important consideration on very long-distance work with perishable goods, especially if crossing mountain ranges was on the cards. *(Photo: Steve Lynch)*

The intercooled DSC11 01 and DSC14 01 were also made available for the bonneted T trucks at the same time as the forward control models. As was the case with R cabs, it was necessary to increase the length of the bonnet by a small amount to accommodate the intercooler unit mounted behind. The extra length was applied to the short snout section in front of the headlights, but it was a far less obvious modification than that applied to the forward control cab.

The perforated SCANIA badge fitted to intercooled R cabs, which allowed a little more air to pass to the radiator, was not a feature of the bonneted trucks with the same engines.

The chasing T cab in this picture is probably not an intercooled example judging by the lack of the badge that was generally fitted at the bottom of the grille. *(Photo: Scania AB)*

Intercity driver, John Bartholomew, did not have to wait long to get his hands on a Scania following the company's extended trial of an R142 (see page 50). Intercity were highly impressed by the big Swede and John, its driver throughout the trial period, was especially keen to add one to the Volvo fleet if he held the keys. However, by the time a purchase was to be made, Scania had introduced the intercooler models and it was felt that the 333 bhp of the 11-litre engine was enough for Intercity's operations.

(Photo: Paul Willis)

Building material supply German style! If you were going to spend your time getting on and off site with a 38-tonne outfit, then Scania's tag axle chassis was one of the best ways of achieving it. The relatively minor extra weight, compared to a 6 x 4 layout, was a small price to pay for the extra traction that could be made available by raising the third axle. Factor in the massive torque of the 142 and this, on the face of it, over-specced vehicle suddenly makes perfect sense.

Seen north of Frankfurt in 1994, this day-cabbed R142H seems to be making excellent progress. *(Photo: Andreas Wolst)*

Initially, and while there was still demand, Scania continued to offer the 388 bhp non-intercooled 142 alongside the more powerful 420 bhp version. This created a logical ladder effect through its top-range 112 and 142 trucks. Scania could now offer representation at 305, 333, 388 and 420 bhp, which offered ample choice for most operators and eventualities.

These two smart example of the non-intercooled variety were part of the small Kent-based fleet of WSM, which expanded from an owner-driver operation started with a 1979 LB141 around this time.

Although not yet having the company's 'WSM' logo emblazoned on the roof deflectors, the distinctive orange-and-white livery did much to mark out the trucks to anyone who knew them.

Note the lovely matching tilt hauled by the Essex-registered and Scantruck-supplied unit, BKJ 28Y. The step-frame box van, however, bears witness to a former life, possibly with Fine Fare supermarkets. *(Photos: Steve Lynch)*

Scania's 'King of the Road' sticker was aptly applied to the bumper of this R142M, but despite its capabilities the title passed to the intercooled version following its introduction. The F89 parked alongside suffered a similar fate in the late 1970s, such was the steady march of progress throughout the decade that saw engine outputs rising all the time. Being different generations of super truck, these two make an interesting comparison. The Volvo's TD120 engine gave 330 bhp and 933 lb/ft of torque in 1970 whereas the original 142, without intercooler, of ten years later could raise those figures by 17.5 and 25 per cent respectively. Significantly, these improvements came with lower engine speeds and better economy too, such was the progress being made by engine designers.

The elderly F89 seems to be doing well in this company. Note the non-original tank that has replaced Volvo's original 90-gallon item which had a propensity to rot out. *(Photo: Steve Lynch)*

The R112H made an ideal base for a drawbar chassis and proved popular in this role with European hauliers. This colourful Greek truck with 5-metre wheelbase looked especially purposeful with its robust looking three-axle trailer in tow. Standard spec for this chassis would have included the GR871 ten-speed range change gearbox and R770 single reduction rear axle.

Far from home, the driver of this example was proud to pose with it while unloading in Nottingham.

Note the chassis lockers and spare wheel carrier fitted to assist long-distance TIR work. *(Photo: Carl Jarman)*

Following the introduction of the intercooler, Scania made the DSC11 01 the standard engine for the R112 and offered the DS11 15 (305 bhp) as an option. The DS11 14 (280 bhp) previously offered in this role was now only available in the P112 where it was an option alongside the DS11 15.

Low-cab P112s with 280 bhp actually represented the upper end of the fleet for Ferrymasters, which considered 250-260 bhp enough for its work. Indeed, when Scania was chasing the company's massive order of 1983 (see page 63) it was being evaluated against Fodens fitted with Cummins 250 bhp LT10 engines and Mercedes-Benz 2025s with a meagre 246 bhp.

(Photo: Steve Lynch)

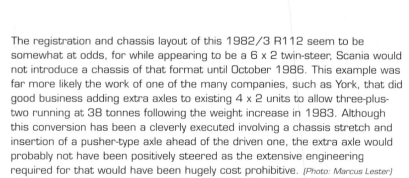

The registration and chassis layout of this 1982/3 R112 seem to be somewhat at odds, for while appearing to be a 6 x 2 twin-steer, Scania would not introduce a chassis of that format until October 1986. This example was far more likely the work of one of the many companies, such as York, that did good business adding extra axles to existing 4 x 2 units to allow three-plus-two running at 38 tonnes following the weight increase in 1983. Although this conversion has been a cleverly executed involving a chassis stretch and insertion of a pusher-type axle ahead of the driven one, the extra axle would probably not have been positively steered as the extensive engineering required for that would have been hugely cost prohibitive. *(Photo: Marcus Lester)*

Scania, for the time being, was sticking resolutely to its trailing axle 6 x 2 chassis to satisfy those of its customers that wanted to operate three-axle tractor units under the new legislation. Scania was a past master at the trailing axle design and although it openly admitted that its 6 x 2s may not couple within the law in every case due to length, it still considered this layout the best way of dealing with 38 tonnes if using a three-axle tractor.

The chassis illustrated, equipped with a bogie lift single tyred trailing axle, was Scania's initial response and was submitted for UK Type Approval early in 1983.

While the first batch of these chassis featured a 3.1 metre wheelbase, Scania soon changed to this 2.85 metre version and made it standard for the UK.

(Photo: Marcus Lester)

Proof positive, if any were needed, that there were some operators that did not require the extra urge of the intercooled 112. As Scania had dropped the 280 bhp engine as an option for the R112, this superb example, with a simple yet effective livery, would have been fitted with the 305 bhp DS11 15, which gave ample power to propel a 32-ton combination on UK work. The engine also provided 911 lb/ft of torque, which would have made for easy and relaxed cruising with fewer gear changes and good fuel returns.

Note the wide axle spread of the trailer. *(Photo: Adrian Cypher)*

Showing stunning attention to detail in its finish, this remarkably handsome R112 was clearly specced for the job in hand. Besides the 333 bhp intercooled engine, the unit also has the large 400-litre diesel tank, which was almost certainly backed up by the optional 205-litre item on the nearside, and Scania's distinctive roof rack, all of which suited the long-distance continental work it undertook.

Being painted, the origins of the under-bumper spoiler are clear in this instance. Whether Scania's decision to fit a sun visor in this position was planned or the result of some accidental discovery is not known, but the items did carry separate part numbers for the different roles.

(Photo: David Wakefield)

Even though it was very much in his blood, Chris Redburn had never really intended to go into haulage and instead pursued a career in music playing bass in the pop group, Kenny. However, both his father and his grandfather were haulage men and when Chris, despite enjoying some chart success, came to understand the fickle nature of the pop music industry he inevitably started to put the two together. After a spell driving for a notable rival, Chris set up Redburn Transfer to service the requirements of bands on tour.

Chris was no stranger to Scanias. His father Jack had operated LB110s in the fleet of H E Dobbs, a concern he had purchased after selling his own haulage company, so it was natural for Chris to opt for a couple of LB111s as his first artics. In 1983, with his fleet now numbering three LB111s and a solitary Volvo, Chris took an R112 demonstrator on a week-long trial from Scantruck. The intercooled truck's arrival coincided with a nice 'local' job hauling Bucks Fizz's gear to Cornwall. Chris was impressed and despite some reservations about the power of the intercooled engine being over and above his requirements, he added A181 POO to his fleet as a result. *(Photo: David Wakefield)*

John Spencer felt the 388 bhp of the non-intercooled R142 was more than adequate for his work and added a second example, seen here on the left, following reliable service from XFD 552X, which by this time had undergone a tag axle conversion to make it a 6 x 2 (see page 36). However, despite being hitched to normal trailers here, the trucks still spent most of their time on plant movement and the third axle was added to allow higher weights in that role rather than to comply with two-axle trailers at 38 tonnes on regular haulage.

Apart from the core business of heavy haulage, Spencer's biggest job was tipping trailers around the UK for SCAC. This resulted in these two trucks and their respective drivers, Bob Taylor and Pete Langley, being based in Portsmouth. The late Pete Langley eventually purchased A830 AMR and put it to work as an owner-driver.

Truck and Trailer conversions of Bristol added the extra axle to both trucks. *(Photo: Adrian Cypher)*

Despite the presence of the intercooler radiator in front of the engine's main coolant item, performance of the latter was unaffected. Even trucks operating on the tough Middle East runs, where desert temperatures would test even the best cooling systems, encountered no direct over-heating problems related to the two units being placed together. Perhaps slightly more worrying for these intrepid drivers was the risk of damage to either unit in the event of a head-on collision, an all too frequent problem thanks to badly driven and often unlit local traffic.

Owner-driver Dave Reynolds worked this R112 for three years on Middle East runs. The truck, under contract to Whittle International, is pictured in Turkey with examples of the basic local transport system, both motorised and un-motorised.

Note the ladder lashed to the air stack.

(Photos: Dave Reynolds)

Newbury-based Sayers Transport operated what was undoubtedly one of the UK's smartest fleets and became synonymous with Scania through the 1970s and '80s. Having started around the turn of the 20th century, Sayers had traditionally run British wagons, including a good number of AECs. The switch to Scania came in 1971 and coincided with the company's first ventures into the bulk powder work at which it was to become a highly regarded specialist, particularly in the supply of raw products for the plastics manufacturing sector in the UK and abroad. The trucks were always highly specced and fitted with numerous extras for comfort and performance, alloy wheels being a common one to off-set the weight of discharge equipment. Despite the odd interloper from Volvo and the A-registered DAF 3300 seen in the line-up on the opposite page, Sayers remained loyal to Scania and found the R112 and R142 perfect for the job. Maintenance, like the livery, was meticulous and was carried out in-house by a dedicated team to a very high standard as, despite Scania's enviable service facilities throughout Europe, breakdowns on what was becoming 'just-in-time' work for process industries could not be tolerated.

Seen heading the line-up in the company's yard – which also includes a smart 1979 LB111 – and inset is A942 AMO, Wessex Gladiator, which was consecutively registered to the unit seen on the right in two very different states. Inevitably, returning trucks would be dirty when the weather was foul, but they would always be thoroughly cleaned before their next trip.

Note the raised leading axle on the trailer of the returning truck, as back-loads were virtually unheard of in this line of work.

(Photos: Marcus Lester & Adrian Cypher)

This smart R112M was something of a rarity in the mainly Volvo fleet of Kammac Trucking. While top weights were rare for this distinctive company on its factory feeder work, the just-in-time nature demanded powerful and reliable tractors. Company chairman, Brian Kamel was a shrewd operator and one of the first to embrace contract hire to significantly increase his fleet at a crucial time, a move that simultaneously allowed him to reduce his stock-holding of spare parts.

Kammac's contract with Salford Van Hire concerned Volvo F10s so the origins of this Scania joining the fleet can only be guessed at.

(Photo: Ashley Coghill)

Like Kammac's, this was another interesting livery, and one that perplexed the author on a previous occasion. Despite his best efforts to identify the company behind this paint scheme as applied to a DAF 3600 Spacecab featured in a previous volume, the company remained unknown. Following publication of the DAF book, a communication from Grahame Austin revealed all. Grahame drove for Rudgewick Transport and Rudgewick's boss, Roy Denton, devised the scheme but a close working relationship with Eddom International, operator of the DAF, saw the livery adopted for its trucks too. It was not uncommon for Grahame to drive Eddom trucks; such was the relationship between the two companies.

This splendid R142 with 6 x 2 chassis was Grahame's regular truck for a number of years. Rudgewick ran two R142s, the other a 4 x 2 unit, on its temperature-controlled work that took the trucks all over mainland Europe amassing annual totals of 70–100,000 miles per unit. *(Photo: David Wakefield)*

Although Scania GB was happy to sell you a spare wheel and tyre when you purchased your 2-series tractor, it did not actually provide a spare wheel carrier for the item or, indeed, list one. Operators that wanted to carry a spare on the unit were left with the option of buying one from another manufacturer and modifying it to suit, fabricating their own or salvaging something from a scrap yard. Chassis space for the item was tight, even on longer wheelbase tractors, and a rear cross-member location would often cause clearance issues with the trailer.

This Belgian operator has gone to great lengths to accommodate a spare, including moving the battery box along, which meant losing the original step above the air tanks and fabricating a new one. The operator must have had good reason for all this work as not only did it incur a hefty weight penalty, but with the position of the auxiliary diesel tank now taken, the truck's effective range was reduced too.

(Photo: Adrian Cypher)

This Iranian R112M was a long way from home when spotted taking a break between Würzburg and Frankfurt in 1999. Much modified, the truck features several items from the 3-series range that was introduced in 1988, including the mirrors and large corner deflectors. The side skirts, however, are of some other origin as are the modifications to the bumper. Heralding from Tehran, the truck was fitted with two number plates, one in Arabic and one legible in Europe. *(Photo: Andreas Wolst)*

Lloyds of Ludlow and Swains of Stretton had both expanded their international activities with earlier Scanias and found the 2-series a natural and logical progression from the reliable LBs they both operated. However, the great breadth of the G P R range and the ease at which an operator could tailor a truck from a basic list of components to suit a specific purpose was bringing new customers to Scania too. In the second year of production UK sales jumped by over 65 per cent with nearly 1,500 trucks sold. Crucially, Scania was gaining sales in the important sectors over 14.5 tonnes and was showing a particular strength in tractor sales with an increase of 4 per cent over the previous year.

The professionalism of these two great UK firms is apparent from the presentation of the vehicles, which made these liveries well known throughout continental Europe.

Note that neither of these companies opted for left-hand drive units and that Swains chose not to have the sleeper window fitted to this impressive R142. *(Photos: David Wakefield)*

Holland, with its compact size and modern road system, actively celebrates the big truck and its people regard it as a positive and essential part of the economy. High gross weights of 50 tonnes were permitted internally and local conditions and regulations gave rise to some interesting configurations such as this 8 x 2 drawbar. Comprising a 32-tonne GVW rigid and three-axle trailer, this became a popular way for Dutch operators to shift two 20 ft ISO containers. However, the eight-wheeler chassis was not unique to Holland and Scania offered many variants in many countries, including an 8 x 4 heavy haulage tractor. In the UK, where the type was most popular for tipper operators, Chas Braham and Sons of Chapletown took delivery of the country's first P82 8 x 4 in 1982.

(Photo: Adrian Cypher)

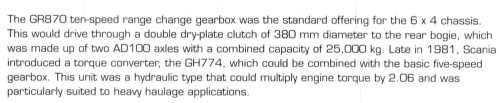

The GR870 ten-speed range change gearbox was the standard offering for the 6 x 4 chassis. This would drive through a double dry-plate clutch of 380 mm diameter to the rear bogie, which was made up of two AD100 axles with a combined capacity of 25,000 kg. Late in 1981, Scania introduced a torque converter, the GH774, which could be combined with the basic five-speed gearbox. This unit was a hydraulic type that could multiply engine torque by 2.06 and was particularly suited to heavy haulage applications.

Although a rather more humble 4 x 2 P112 is illustrated, it was the heavy haulage concern of J B Rawcliffe & Sons that in 1982 took delivery of the first UK example to be fitted with the torque converter. It is not known if Norman Keedwell's splendid R142 was so equipped.

Note the super singles fitted to the front of Norman's truck and the non-original diesel tank.

(Photos: Clive Davies & Ashley Coghill)

The 142 as a factory trailing axle tractor like this carried the full designation of R142MA 6 x 2 RC05. The layout proved popular for those operators, such as Christopher Miners, on the more arduous of long-distance continental work and beyond where the tractor's weight would be offset by its superb durability and the traction benefits afforded by the lift axle. However, for the same operators, the biggest problem with this chassis format was the short 2.85-metre wheelbase, which only allowed room for the 300-litre diesel tank. Costly chassis modifications to the batteries and air tanks could make room for an additional tank on the left of the chassis, but most opted to fit catwalk diesel tanks like this to improve range.

Note the non-original, striped seat covers fitted to this superb example and the glorious and robust tilt by the French manufacturer Trailor. *(Photos: Marcus Lester)*

John William Harold Spicer started his haulage firm in 1932. The company evolved over the years mixing general haulage with a solid-fuel business. When his sons became involved it was Peter, the younger one, who took over the running of the haulage side, including responsibility for the coal trucks and the workshop, while Eric ran the solid fuel from the paperwork side.

Peter had some fresh ideas about how to operate and built a happy and successful family business by providing a dedicated number of trucks to essentially three good customers, which paid over the odds for his guaranteed availability. He also knew what he wanted from a truck and, following terrible support from Leyland which resulted in him travelling to the factory one night a week for many years to collect what he needed in the way of spares for his fleet, he began to look at alternatives. A brief and unhappy dalliance with Mercedes proved little better. However, an early LB110, which Peter travelled to Scotland to collect – as it was the only one available in the country – sold him on Scania and from then on no other manufacturer was ever considered.

The fleet ran to sixteen tractor units for haulage, including one spare at all times to cover servicing, which was religiously and meticulously carried out every 5,000 miles. The trucks also featured Autolube systems from new. The resulting condition of the units was so good that they held the pass record at the Royston testing station and Ro-Truck, Stowmarket were quick to buy every truck, plus all the trailers, when Peter sold up in 1993.

This unit was one of two R142s that was operated alongside R and P112s and was driven by the late Des Greene. The tilt trailer belonged to Cobelfreight, a regular customer, via Harwich. Contents could be anything, but a mere six-tons of Pampers nappies was not uncommon. However, back loads were generally steel on this contract. *(Photo: Marcus Lester)*

Walker & Son and Lawsons are two prime examples of that rather special sector within the haulage industry, family firms that have survived and prospered. Both were established in the early 1950s and both maintain a fleet of around fifty trucks. Although largely into general haulage, both have specialist divisions for crane hire and other activities. The key to survival, it would seem, is customer service, flexibility through size, impeccable presentation and above all, reliability.

Naturally, for companies starting out in the 1950s, both ran English trucks initially, but were swayed in the following decades by the superior imports, particularly from Sweden.

Here the company's buying policies seemed to be perfectly aligned with R112M 6 x 2s. The Walker truck makes a refreshing sight compared to the usual tilts and reefers streaming through Dover. Lawsons is seen at rest in the company's Cockermouth yard. *(Photos: David Wakefield & John W Henderson)*

What would Jim McKelvie, the man who established Volvo trucks in the UK, have made of this? Simple: recognising the benefits afforded to the haulier by the extensive nature of the G P R truck range and the modular system, he would have applauded it wholeheartedly. Of course, McKelvie had long since sold the family haulage firm to the TDG, but the fact remains that as a shrewd businessman and luminary of road haulage, he would have recognised the great potential of the 2-series and, one suspects, particularly the P112, which offered big truck performance in a smaller and cheaper package.

(Photo: Marcus Lester)

Woolwich-based B J Myers ran a mainly DAF fleet in the early 1980s with a smattering of Volvos, Mercs, MANs and Scanias. Following the introduction of the 38-tonne limit, the company, which specialised in tipping continental trailers throughout the UK, adopted a policy of running three-axle units. This was not only better for flexibility in that any unit could take any trailer, be it two- or three-axle, but as drivers were not privy to the loading of incoming trailers, it was also a safeguard against the possibility of drive axle overloads on a 4 x 2 unit.

The company initially converted a number of its DAFs with Granning lift axles before settling on twin-steers from a number of manufacturers once that format became available. However, This P112M would appear to be a factory 6 x 2, judging by the short wheelbase, which provided Myers with a good and reasonably low weight solution in the early days of 38-tonne operation.

(Photo: Steve Lynch)

A consideration for some operators when looking to purchase a 2-series tractor was the height of the cab. This could be of particular importance to those involved in tipper and bulk work where the requirement to fit under hoppers and farm building entrances, the latter originally designed for little more than loaded horse carts, was a frequent occurrence. The R cab, although not the tallest – that crown going to the Transcontinental as far as a standard cab was concerned – was certainly among the biggest of the premium tractors at the time measuring nearly 3.5 metres to the top of the air stack. By comparison, the P cab was nearly a foot shorter.

Richards & Osborne Ltd ran at least three consecutively registered P112Ms on its tipper and general haulage operations out of Cornwall, most of which featured the deep-section catwalk diesel tank visible here on these two hard-worked examples. *(Photos: Marcus Lester)*

Perhaps it is accentuated by the rather deep frame section of the skeletal trailer in this instance, but this P112M does seem a little dwarfed by the ISO-dimensioned fridge box it is hauling here. Although allowing a plentiful supply of fresh air to the chiller unit, the air resistance must have been immense, especially at motorway speeds. No doubt the driver noticed reduced performance and a rapidly dropping fuel gauge. However, even the factory air management kit would have failed to bridge the gap properly between truck and trailer height on this occasion.

Note how the chiller unit is contained within the ISO dimensions by the frame of the box. *(Photo: Marcus Lester)*

By comparison, the container and skelly combination hauled by this R142 sits much better aesthetically. While the lucky driver of this 420 bhp unit would have been hard pushed to notice any discernible difference in performance caused by varying trailer heights, even the R142 would have recorded a drop in mpg if hauling a trailer with a height gap as pronounced as that of the P112 above. Although this unit also lacked any of the factory wind-cheating aides, the windscreen rake and the sun visor alone would have started to move the air in a beneficial manner to overcome the minor height difference between the cab roof and trailer. *(Photo: Marcus Lester)*

If necessity is indeed the mother of invention, then legislation is a cruel mistress. Whichever way you looked at it, this 6 x 2 solution was not a pretty one and categorically flew in the face of that old engineering adage 'if it looks right, it is right'. However, what choice did Scania, champion of the 6 x 2 tag axle, have at the time? In the wake of the increase to 38 tonnes, truck manufacturers wrestled with ways to accommodate the growing requirement for three-axle tractor units without adding too much weight. Buyers, with no operational experience of the new weight, swithered and dithered about how best to move forward. To get the decision wrong and opt for the solution that did not gain universal acceptance would have been like choosing Betamax rather than VHS (ask your parents if you are under 35) with crippling financial results. Re-engineering its 6 x 2 chassis was a logical step for Scania and one that did not commit the company to expensive tooling changes. Essentially this configuration utilised a twin-tyred axle beam with the outer wheels removed. The only change concerned the balance beam between the drive and tag axle, which was redesigned to give a new and appropriate ratio.

(Photos: Adrian Cypher and Marcus Lester)

The Lock fleet, around 20-strong in the late 1980s, was made up of second-hand units from MAN, DAF, Scania, ERF and Seddon Atkinson. The trucks were all ADR-compliant with full pet-reg equipment including front-mounted exhausts, shrouded air stacks and full engine partitioning. This work, as now, was always carried out by Lock's own fitters and even extended to the removal of factory stereo systems and the installation of a 24-volt non-return earth radio.

At the time, Lock's trucks were generally assigned to specific jobs and drivers were moved around. Paul Willis enjoyed a two-month stint at the wheel of this R112M in the late 1980s. The factory 6 x 2 trailing axle layout gave a superb ride and the 333 bhp was still more than up to the task of 38-tonne work throughout the UK. Company policy did change later on, at which point Paul was allocated a MAN, probably ex-SAMAS of Liverpool, as his regular truck.

Still going strong in 2013, Lock now buys its trucks new. *(Photos: Paul Willis)*

Given the intense rivalry between Volvo and Scania, it is maybe surprising that the 2-series was not offered with a high roof extension. The Globetrotter was launched in 1979 following a very secretive development period – Volvo even exercised a no-fly zone over its test track. This left little time for Scania to accommodate such radical changes in its own designs for the G P R cabs, which had been finalised and given tooling approval under 'Project Q' in May 1977. The only other pointer to the 'high rise' trend that would sweep through the industry in the following years was the very limited edition, and not factory produced, offering from Berliet, so Scania can be forgiven for missing the boat on this occasion.

Although a cheap and easy solution may have been possible using GFRP, like the later Spacecab from DAF, Scania would not have entertained such a construction as it would never have met Swedish crash criteria and would have then been unavailable to its home market.

After-market additions were, of course, up to the buyer as is illustrated by this rather neat conversion to a Dutch registered R142, and numerous companies sprang up to supply the gap in the market. *(Photos: Steve Lynch & Adrian Cypher)*

A367 KKK started out new with Barrio in 1984. The Sittingbourne-based company purchased the R142M to run as an evaluation vehicle against an F12 Globetrotter. Following the trial, which did not spur any further purchases of Scanias for Barrio, the unit was sold to fellow Kent haulier, WSM. Although W S Motors had the odd Volvo – one is seen in the background here – its eggs were, more or less, placed in the basket labelled 'Scania' and had been since its early days with an LB141. The 420 bhp unit was fitted with the full air management package and the view of it in WSM's colours shows the breathing hole in the side screen that still allowed the air stack an uninterrupted supply of air.

Note the back end of an old Guy Big J in the Barrio yard picture. This was an ex-Intercity unit and veteran of many a cross-channel adventure. *(Photos: Mark Robinson)*

The intercooled engine was standard for the R142 in the E chassis, rather than an option as it was in the M and H. These capable Econofreight examples with hub reduction 6 x 4 layouts would probably have also featured the optional torque converter. In this configuration, Scania rated the rear bogie capacity as 30,000 kg and allowed a GTW of 150 tons.

The massive Lancer Linde H420 forklift being transported here was part of the company's Hermes range. Capable of handling loads of up to 40 tonnes this behemoth was ideal for container movements and proved popular on docksides around the world. As it stood, minus fork carriage etc, it weighed in at a hefty 38,112 kg. Factor in its length/width/height dimensions of 7.80 x 3.56 x 3.96 metres and you have load worthy of the specialist abilities of a firm such as Econofreight.

Note the optional headlight wash-wipe in the close-up photo and the different design of front towing hitch applied to each truck.

(Photos: Marcus Lester & Peter Davison)

It is doubtful that the engineering brilliance of Brunel was wasted on the Scania PR department when this glorious photograph was staged with the Royal Albert Bridge, Saltash – one of the great man's finest achievements – in the background. Would there have been mutual respect? Absolutely. The ability of a machine with one driver to shift a 20-tonne payload many hundreds of miles in a day without the constriction of rails would certainly have had the Victorian engineer doffing his incredibly tall hat, although he may well have had something to say about its impact on his beloved railways! *(Photo: Scania AB)*

When a company kept its trucks as long as Gallacher Bros did with these two examples, the initially higher price of the Scania product was easily recouped following the years of extra service that resulted from the general robust nature of the trucks. When John W Henderson visited the company yard in 1998, this pair were getting on for 14 years old, were clearly both well worked and had doubtless paid for themselves many times over.

The P112 was originally purchased new and operated as a 6 x 2 unit at 38 tonnes alongside similar offerings from DAF and Leyland (Scammell). The origin of the R142 is not known, but it did appear in a company line-up in 1985 so may also have been purchased new, perhaps as part of the same deal.

Note the after-market air deflector that was fitted to the R142 in later life and the silver bumpers, a marked move away from the hazard-striped finish originally applied and which was once a trademark of this company's smart livery. *(Photos: John W Henderson)*

Truck manufacturers that make all the major components in-house have a clear advantage over rivals that do not because each part is engineered to work with the next; engines match gearboxes, match axles – there is no compromise.

This, combined with the inherent strength and durability of Scania components generally, made second-hand 2-series trucks highly sought after, particularly those coming from well-known fleets with impeccable service records, which in this case looks likely to have been Swains of Stretton.

Note the catwalk diesel tank and GLC exemption sticker on this example. *(Photo: Adrian Cypher)*

Despite the extensive wind tunnel testing of half-scale models in the development period of the cab, the 2-series still suffered rather more mirror and side window fouling than was desirable. This inherent problem for trucks is generally caused by dirt getting caught up in the turbulence generated by the front wheel nuts. Scania did address this in the design of the G P R cab in the form of slots running behind the bulges of the corner panels. These created a strong air stream at a height intended to carry away the dirt. However, with customer feedback suggesting more could be done, Scania developed additional corner panels for the later 3-series, a pair of which has been retro-fitted here.

(Photo: Adrian Cypher)

The G P R cab interior came in four trim levels of comfort class: A, B, C and D. For the UK and Europe, only A and B were available, the more basic C and D being intended for developing countries. Comfort class A offered the driver a very pleasant and sumptuous place to work with features such as a sprung and heated seat, air conditioning, night heater, twin bunks, electric passenger window and a stereo cassette with three speakers. The top package also included exterior items such as the sun visor. Colours were a combination of dark browns and beige, making the interior warm and cosy. *(Photo: Scania AB)*

While enjoying the luxury interior and revelling in the Scania performance, the lucky 2-series driver was also aware that the cab was one of the strongest and safest on the market. Swedish impact tests demanded that cab doors remained shut and serviceable following a 1-ton weight being swung into the A-pillars and back panel. It also had to be strong enough to support a static 15-ton weight on the roof.

No doubt the driver was thankful for all that strength after this example ended up on its side.

Note that the M on the badge has, for some reason, been reversed to read W. *(Photo: Peter Davison)*

Mazo, which operated around 120 trucks at the time of these photos, was one of the most prolific Spanish operators in Europe and, although now running with a modified livery, its trucks are still a common sight on the continent's roads. By specialising in the movement of fruit, particularly to the UK and Germany, the mixed fleet of Pegasos, Scanias and MANs was kept very busy. These intercooled 142s represented the most powerful trucks on the fleet at the time and were typically European in their spec. The long wheelbases allowed a large diesel tank to be mounted on the right of the chassis and a spare wheel and carrier, fitted to all Mazo trucks, on the left. The extensive journeys up through Europe would see Mazo trucks clocking 120-130,000 miles annually and units were generally renewed after three or four years. The distinctive SOR fridge trailers with Carrier chiller units, featured a lifting front axle for light and empty running.

Note the roof-mounted air deflector, which was an after-market item also fitted to the company's Pegaso and MAN tractors.

(Photos: Adrian Cypher and Paul Willis)

Scania has always taken the quality of components very seriously, after all it was quality that set the trucks apart from most of the competition. Constant analysis of the current range had always been a part of the company's ethos and the 2-series was no different. Research and development was always ongoing and one in ten employees were actively involved in quality control. When the 2-series was current, in addition to lab testing, Scania had a staggering 5,000 trucks undergoing field trials with operators around the world and any changes made from the findings were filtered through to the customer in the shape of improved components.

This splendid R112 6 x 2 worked in Carpenters' small and largely Volvo fleet alongside a Y-registered R142.

Note the aluminium wheels fitted to this unit, which gave a useful weight saving of around 150 kg on the 6 x 2 chassis. *(Photos: Adrian Cypher & Simon Carpenter)*

The 2-series came equipped with two powerful halogen headlights as standard. The 2-series marked Scania's return to square headlights, which had been ousted by round units since the first face-lift was made to the LB110 in 1973. Unlike the rectangular units of the original LB110, which had a poor reputation for forward lighting, these expensive items were more than up to the job and many found it unnecessary to augment them with the optional spotlights. Mimicking the location of the later LB models, the units were mounted above the bumper and were set back to protect them. A very useful feature of the units was the on-board adjuster that allowed the driver to alter the beam height from inside the cab to compensate for different loadings on the back. *(Photo: John W Henderson)*

A headlight wash–wipe facility was law for trucks sold in Sweden so, having developed it, Scania made it available to other markets as an optional extra. Despite the benefits of the system, it was not widely specified by operators. However, this rather unusual fish transporter does have it fitted, the short wiper arm being just visible on the left-hand unit. It also features not only spotlights in the factory-provided apertures, but an additional set in cutouts made after delivery. All of which suggests that this truck regularly encountered poor visibility, perhaps from mist on low-lying fish farms.

The incredible span of the 2-series G P R range meant that this highly specialised truck was constructed on a virtually stock chassis.

Note the deep lockers required to house the essential aeration equipment for the tanks.

(Photo: David Wakefield)

Although he did not operate an exclusively Scania fleet, Peter Hinchcliffe rated them highly and would buy eight to ten units a year as part of the constant cycle that kept his thirty-strong fleet in tip-top condition. The trucks were always supplied by Graham Commercials, which was based nearby on the same Carlisle industrial estate. The immaculate presentation and numbers of Scanias operated led to a very good relationship with the manufacturer and Hinchcliffe vehicles would feature in Scania literature from time to time.

Coal from the opencast mines of Lanarkshire made up much of the work, but Hinchcliffe trucks also handled a lot of wheat and malting barley, much of which was unloaded at Leith docks in Edinburgh where B819 JHH is pictured. The trucks would also run abroad, often taking out loads of non-ferrous metal destined for Holland and back-loading with foundry coke from northern France. *(Photos: John W Henderson & David Wakefield)*

Lawson's found that even the challenging topography of Cumbria was easily tamed by the DSC11 01 engine with its generous 1025 lb/ft of torque, even at 38 tonnes. When *Commercial Motor* put an intercooled R112 around its test route in 1983 it demonstrated a devastating hill-storming ability when it charged up Carter Bar in an impressive time of 4.28 minutes, without the need of a down change in the ten-speed box. Lawson's celebrated the topography of its Cockermouth location with fleet names all starting with 'Mountain'.

This stunning example was virtually new at the time of this photograph.

[Photo: John W Henderson]

While the DSC11 01 in the R112 impressed with its hill-climbing ability, the mighty DSC14 01 was a revelation to drivers at the time. As a general haulage truck, the engine's huge torque curve was enough to power a fully freighted example over most obstacles without dropping a gear, which made the truck both quick and economical. *Truck* magazine demonstrated the truck's storming performance during a road test in1984, in which it despatched the tough M18/M1 section from Doncaster to Derby in 67.5 minutes.

With different gearing and drive, this mountain of torque could also be tailored for extreme heavy haulage as here.

[Photo: Adrian Cypher]

Although at the time its fleet was largely made up of Seddon Atkinson and ERF units, Leggett did not operate a purely British buying policy, it just considered that the domestic products were generally as good as any other. Foreign trucks were tried from time to time, including Volvo and DAF, but none really impressed until a batch of six R112s were purchased for 38-tonne operation.

This unit spent much of its time working out of Leggett's Bredbury depot on a regular night trunk to Enfield, North London. Lawrence Chapman enjoyed 18 months at the wheel and found it a far cry from his first truck with the firm, an Atkinson Borderer with day cab, which he used to drive to Switzerland regularly. *(Photo: Carl Jarman)*

Although this unit was produced after the UK weight increase, many an operator was pleased to find that earlier examples needed no upgrading to handle the new weights, even 4 x 2 units had more than enough extra capacity within the original design.

Being a great fan of the company's earlier DAFs, the author makes no secret of his admiration for Robin East's superb Rokold fleet and its subtle livery, which looks remarkably good here applied to the big R cab. *(Photo: David Wakefield)*

1984 was another record year for Scania in the UK with sales of 2,501 trucks exceeding predictions and smashing the previous year's total of 1,929 by a considerable margin. While the recovering market was showing an increase of 11 per cent in the 15-tonne plus sector, Scania's own growth was an impressive 31.5 per cent.

Key to this growth was the valuable fleet sales that had largely eluded Scania with the old LB range. Among the important 'blue chip' companies investing in Scanias, and which other firms watched for buying trends, were Ryder Truck Rental, BRS, P & O, Lex Wilkinson, Russell Davies and British Airways. Also included was TNT

which actively advised and encouraged its sub-contractors, such as D J Ponsonby & Sons, which ran a number of R112s as a result of the TNT connection.

Note how big the 400-litre tank looks on this P-cabbed tractor. *(Photo: Clive Davies)*

The transport of peat from the Somerset levels was big business for R T Keedwell. This unit is pictured at Godwins' peat works at Westhay, but the company's biggest customer was Fisons and it was the loss of this business to Russell Davies that hit Keedwells so hard in the early 1990s. The fleet dropped to just twelve units as a result, but a monumental comeback followed and now, in 2013, the fleet is nearly 500-strong!

The very short wheelbase of this chassis made for a super-manoeuvrable unit that could turn on the proverbial sixpence when the tag axle was lifted, but such activity with a trailer on the back, particularly a three-axle one, would wreak havoc with its tyres.

(Photo: Clive Davies)

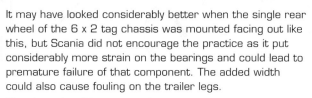

It may have looked considerably better when the single rear wheel of the 6 x 2 tag chassis was mounted facing out like this, but Scania did not encourage the practice as it put considerably more strain on the bearings and could lead to premature failure of that component. The added width could also cause fouling on the trailer legs.

Note how the side window of the sleeper has been covered over with the livery – its rubber being clearly visible – and the broken lower step. *(Photo: Clive Davies)*

The need for airlines to move air-cargo containers between European airports gave rise to all sorts of interesting trucks appearing in the 1980s. Truck manufacturers and bodywork companies stretched the boundaries in a desperate attempt to accommodate the 'holy grail' of five such containers. The close-coupled drawbar became king in this sector and there were a number of high-bred truck/bus chassis used. A top sleeper for the driver was virtually essential in these roles as cabs were often further shortened versions of day cabs. Dutch companies became particularly adept at creating roof pods with a particularly notable one, Estepe, being established in 1984, right in the middle of 2-series production.

Note that this truck has intercooler badges, but not the intercooler cab profile? *(Photo: Adrian Cypher)*

Maybe not quite so specialised, but still following the max-cube principal, this R112 looks mighty impressive too. For Harry Vos, both Scania and de-mountable bodies have played a significant role. Established following liberation by the allies in 1944, Harry Vos grew his company quickly. When hostilities finished in 1945 his trucks became very busy with the rebuilding of the Holland's infrastructure. Scanias arrived in the '60s and have been popular with the company ever since, while de-mountable bodies were adopted for the efficiency and speed at which trucks could be turned around with other pre-loaded ones. *[Photo: Adrian Cypher]*

Roba's experience with early Volvo twin-steer tractors was not a favourable one and strengthened Scania's stance on sticking with its existing 6 x 2 tag chassis to meet the new requirements of hauliers wanting to operate three-axle tractors, rather than rushing through a new design.

However, Scania's 6 x 2 was too long for some operators like Roba, so despite its allegiance, it was forced to look elsewhere. Apart form an unusual number of engine failures, Roba found its Volvos had a massive appetite for tyres. This was mostly attributed to the second steering axle relieving the drive axle of

too much weight allowing it to spin, which may also have caused the engines to over-rev. Volvo would ultimately develop its twin-steer into a successful design, while Scania took its time to assess what was operationally required. *(Photo: Paul Willis)*

Honeybourne Haulage Ltd was a small operation that grew from John Foster's original owner-operator set-up which he started in 1973. A great deal of the company's work involved the night-time movement of road planers and other plant associated with highway repair and resurfacing. The yellow livery was adopted for safety reasons in that environment. Other work included hay and straw, poultry and the movement of peat. The latter was seasonal and intense.

This well-worked R112 was one of three 2-series Scanias operated by John and it completed around 18 years' service.

Note the generous locker under the trailer.

(Photo: Clive Davies)

In 1984 the Brewery Transport Advisory Committee organised the IRTE annual fuel economy test for trucks at the MIRA proving ground. Scania entered a stock R112, taken from its current demonstration fleet, for the 38-tonne category and won with an impressive figure of 8.12 mpg. In doing this it beat a number of 'factory' prepared trucks from other manufacturers. Scania knew it could achieve a good result without special preparation and wanted parity with operators' own figures as an unrealistic result would have raised awkward questions from its customers.

Figures like that for mpg would have been especially important to companies like Fenton's when faced with the long haul down into England. *(Photo: David Kay)*

Although Scania constantly developed the 2-series during its production life, it resisted any re-designation and retained the original 82, 112 and 142 model identification numbers. This was something the company was well practised at. Even the rather significant alterations that were made to the LB110 in 1973, which saw the headlights changed to circular items and re-positioned in the grille, went un-announced by a new model number. However, detail improvements and the introduction of new features were ongoing. For example, gearboxes were up-rated in the summer of 1983, the GR870 becoming the GR871 and the GS770 replaced by two alternatives with different ratios, the GS771 and GS772. It also introduced a gearbox oil cooler for use in some applications.

Note the R cabbed 3-series unit parked alongside, identifiable by the low-level air stack of the later model.
(Photo: John W Henderson)

The 420 bhp of the intercooled V8 put Scania in a unique position for a European manufacturer in one of the world's toughest trucking environments, Australia. The prodigious output of the DSC14 01 allowed the big Scania to tackle maximum-weight road train operations legally with three trailers at 118 tonnes, a sector dominated by high-powered, if unsophisticated, American trucks at the time. As Scania did not have a gearbox with a low enough crawler gear, it was necessary for these

prime movers to be locally fitted with alternatives, more often than not a Fuller item. However, various operators were chosen to test a prototype Scania box designated the GRS871, and while it would seem that this unit did not make production, the information gained during the field trials in Australia was almost certainly used in the development of the GRS900, a combined range and splitter type gearbox, which would become generally available on the later 3-series.

Although this smart R112 was not operating at anything like the 118 tonnes of Australian-spec 142s, and was too early to have benefited from the GRS900 gearbox, numerous minor improvements would have been incorporated into its design. These would have come from Scania's experiences with 2-series trucks in its world markets since the range was originally launched.

Note the front mud flaps, very Australian! *(Photo: Paul Willis)*

Strictly speaking, the 92, much like the 82, is actually outside the scope of a book that concentrates on the 112 and 142. However, the author felt that one example should be included as the model did represent an important addition to the already vast G P R T range, and it was particularly significant for UK operators still operating below the 38-tonne maximum, of which there were many.

Far more than just an 82 with a bored-out engine, the 92 was very much a model in its own right and actually featured an all-new engine that shared no common parts with the old 8-litre unit. Another six-cylinder design, with an extra 700 cc over the DS8, the new 8.5 litre engine was available in two states of tune, the 245 bhp DS9 01 and the 275 bhp DSC9 01. The DSC was an intercooled type, but unlike the intercooled engine available in the 82, the new engine shared the air-to-air system of the bigger engines and as such, trucks fitted with it featured extended front grille and corner panels, as seen here.

The 92 was launched in 1984 following two years of extensive field trials which amounted to over two million miles in the UK alone. A number of trusted operators were asked to take part in the field trials with trucks badged up as 82s, although Russell Davies thought the improved performance might arouse some suspicion and fitted a 112 badge to its example.

A significant factor with the 92 was its ability to be supplied with the R cab, which widened its appeal to operators, especially those running long-distance services but not necessarily at maximum weights. Pollock's fine example was fitted with the P cab, but was built on the heavy chassis. The truck was purchased in the late 1980s following a career with Deptford-based Robson Road Haulage, a staunch Scania user, where it had been used on the distribution of Holsten Pils and other fine beverages.

(Photo: John W Henderson)

Scania introduced a new pattern of diesel tank towards the end of UK C-registrations in the first half of 1986. Although the capacities remained the same as before, the new items featured a softer radius, different cap locations and the distinct end pressing visible here. Although a part of the ongoing development and improvement of the 2-series, these items actually represented the early introduction of 3-series components.

Thomas Smith Jnr was originally involved in the transportation of fish, for which its location in Leith, Edinburgh's harbour town, was ideal. However, the company made a shift to the more glamorous, though potentially dangerous, whisky haulage sector in the 1960s.

Photographed in 1987, a unit with trailer is seen parked outside the company's Pitt Street depot while a solo unit waits inside the workshop behind. Both of these trucks feature the company's revised livery of 1985 and also have the top of the range blue cab interior, which was first introduced in 1984 as the A trim for the R cab only. The top spec cab featured Isringhausen suspension seats, double bunks, carpeted engine tunnel and curtains and panelling all finished in a gentle blue. Although ERF had marketed a blue interior for its old B-series, Scania's inspiration for the new colour was probably inspired by Renault, which had adopted it for its top of the range R370 the previous year. Scania received a gold medal from the British Carriage and Automobile Manufacturers for the blue cab package when it was showcased, along with the new 92 range, at the NEC Motor Show in 1984. *(Photos: John W Henderson)*

The introduction of the DS9 gave the 2-series an impressive output coverage from 188 to 420 bhp from its 7, 8, 8.5, 11 and 14-litre engines. In the summer of 1985, Scania decided that the non-intercooled version of the 14-litre engine was no longer required. Intercooling had proved very successful not just for the increased power it offered, but also the improved reliability and engine life that the engine enjoyed by virtue of the lower thermal loadings. Two intercooled versions of the 14-litre engine were made available at this point with ratings of 390 and 420 bhp, though a change to ISO measuring allowed Scania to claim 400 and 430 bhp which, in the later case, was enough to usurp the new Italian pretender, the Iveco TurboStar 420.

While progress is inevitable, many were sad to see the passing of the turbo-only V8 after sixteen years of production. *(Photo: Marcus Lester)*

Scania made a major technological leap in 1984/5 with the introduction of its CAG, Computer Aided Gearshifting system, which marked the arrival of electronic control in trucks. The system used a computer to process information from sensors reading various aspects of speed, engine output and gear selection to advise the driver of the required changes, which were then made by just depressing the clutch. The CAG system was first shown to UK customers at the 1984 British International Show when its cost was just over £1,700.

It is unlikely that this impressive outfit was equipped with CAG, but given the subsequent development and adoption of automatic transmissions in the years since, its modern-day equivalent might well be.

(Photo: Clive Davies)

The beauty of Scania's CAG system was that it could be applied to a standard driveline. Besides the control unit and sensors the only other hardware was the air actuators that performed the actual shift in the standard manual gearbox. So, although it was initially aimed at distribution vehicles and coach/bus chassis, the system was gradually made available across the

entire range up to and including the 142. The system was simple and could be overridden by the driver if road situations demanded it. A small box with a control switch and a paddle type joystick, which allowed the driver to make up and down changes manually if required, replaced the normal gear stick. The removal of the conventional lever and linkages could actually

save weight, which in the case of a rear-engined coach chassis could as much as 100 lb.

Again, it is unlikely that this magnificent R142 was fitted with anything other than the standard GR871 gearbox, but potentially it could have had the CAG system. *(Photo: Marcus Lester)*

To cater for the potential performance of the 142, Scania were generous when designing the braking system for the 2-series. The dual circuit system employed massive ten-inch drums on rear axles and seven-inch drums on the front, which gave a three-axle unit like this a total braking area of 1,227 inches squared. The parking brake would activate on the front and drive axle in all cases irrespective of the total number of axles. All tractor units and drawbar rigids were fitted with a separate trailer brake which was activated by a dash-mounted lever, and all trucks had an exhaust brake. Both of these additional devices could be used on long descents to preserve the trucks's brakes.

Note the headlight protection grilles fitted to this anonymous example. *(Photo: Clive Davies)*

This two-axled drawbar chassis used the same 10- and 7-inch drum set-up as the three-axle chassis, which gave a braking area of 948 inches squared. Two-axled trucks, rigid or tractor, were fitted with four air reservoirs, two of 16-litre capacity and two of 27-litre capacity. Three-axled trucks were fitted with an extra 27-litre tank. The braking system was plumbed in rust-protected steel or high-impact synthetics, which made it both durable and easy to service. The exhaust brake, which was standard across the entire 2-series range, was particularly effective on the bigger-capacity engines, especially the 14-litre.

Note the spare wheel carrier and the very high drop sides of the trailer on this Swedish-operated example.

(Photo: Adrian Cypher)

At the time of writing, during the closing weeks of 2013, this plucky P112, originally part of Keedwell's brick and block fleet, was still putting in a regular day's work as a yard shunter for the Somerset haulier. With nearly thirty years of continuous service, it provides proof positive, if any were needed, of the remarkable strength and reliability of the 2-series. Scania were often criticised by jealous rivals for the higher purchase price of its trucks and the unladen weight, which was higher than most competitors, but both of these were symptomatic of the quality engineering that could produce service life such as this.

Note the replacement battery lid, which looks very much like a Volvo item. *(Photo: Clive Davies)*

The W H Malcolm haulage business consisted of a single truck and a horse and cart when Donald Malcolm took it over at the tender age of fourteen. With great fortitude he built the company up over the next forty years to the point, during the heyday of the 2-series, when W H Malcolm operated the largest fleet in Scotland with close on 400 trucks. These were driven, cared for and organised by an equally impressive workforce numbering around 600. Scanias had been prolific in the fleet for many years with the LB110/111 proving particularly popular following good experience with the original LB76. Although other makes, including Volvo, were also well represented, it was the 112 in both R and P cab that the company virtually standardised on in this period as Donald considered the mix of reliability and economy to be just about perfect. He also found that the Scanias provided the best tyre wear on the fleet. Most of the company's Scanias were purchased new from Reliable Vehicles, but good second-hand examples were always considered. Donald's opinion of his Scanias was such that the company actively started to restore its old LB111s with brand-new cabs to extend their working lives in the late 1980s.

The late R112 on the left makes an interesting comparison with the early P113 alongside it, while the truck on the right was far from home when photographed heading towards the West Country. Although servicing, which was carried out in-house, was meticulous, company policy ensured that vehicles travelling so far from home were generally less than three years old.

Note the new battery box and air tank arrangement that started to appear at this time, which, like the diesel tanks, were essentially 3-series items and layout making an early appearance.

(Photos: Peter Davison & Marcus Lester)

Scania, in the wake of the new 38-tonne limit for UK operators, had proved beyond doubt that its various 6 x 2 chassis were right for those that wanted a three-axle unit to comply with the new regulations. In the first year of 38-tonne operation, nearly 36 per cent of its sales for tractor units in the over 29-tonne sector were for 6 x 2s. However, although it consistently made up one-third of three-axle tractor sales in the following years, by 1985 it was becoming clear that the industry was definitely starting to favour the twin-steer arrangement as offered by most other manufacturers by that time.

The smart 2-series Scanias of the Hammond fleet were a mix of 4 x 2 and 6 x 2, giving the company the flexibility to run two plus three or three plus two axle combinations as was appropriate.

(Photos: Steve Lynch)

Although for the first quarter of 1986 Scania increased its European sales figure by ten per cent, its UK sales were actually down for the first time in many years. To be fair, the over 29-tonne GCW sector was showing a small drop in general, but in all probability, with a market that was fast adopting the twin-steer tractor, Scania now had an unsatisfactory gap in its extensive range. Luckily, by then the company was in the advanced stages of being able to provide its own solution and announced its twin-steer chassis in October that year.

This superb early example was waiting to tip at a cold store in Salford. *(Photo: Carl Jarman)*

The new twin-steer chassis was classified as a 6 x 2/4 by Scania to save confusion with its trailing axle chassis that was simply referred to as a 6 x 2. The full model designation of this smart example would have been R112 MA 6 x 2/4 RC O5. To break that down for explanation: R – R cab, 11-litre engine, series 2; M – medium chassis; A – tractor (artic); 6 x 2/4 – twin steer; RC – right-hand drive, intercooled (chargecooled); O5 – current level of engine development (theoretically running from 1 to 99).

The standard spec for this model included GR871 range change gearbox and the R770 rear axle fitted with 3.50 to 1 ratio. This gave a geared maximum of 70.5 mph. Fitting the optional 3.89 to 1 ratio dropped that to 63.5 mph, but increased gradeability by 3 per cent, allowing a first-gear ascent of a 1 in 3.3 obstacle at 38 tonnes.

This picture gives a great view of how much tidier the new battery and air tank arrangement was. Note the small Scania badge, probably of coach origin, which has been mounted at the bottom of the grille in place of the intercooler badge. *(Photo: Clive Davies)*

Scania's twin steer may have been a little late to the party, but when it arrived it was, predictably, a superbly engineered and well thought out design, and far more than just a standard long chassis with an extra steering axle hung off it. In fact, the chassis was unique and specifically engineered for the purpose.

Classified as M (medium) it should not be confused with the M spec chassis of the trailing axle 6 x 2, although its design capacity was the same at 51.2 ton. To counter the extra weight that would be inevitable with the addition of the extra steering axle and its attendant mechanisms, the new chassis was constructed with

side members of 8.0 mm thickness, as used on the 4 x 2 M chassis, in place of the 9.5 mm items of the 6 x 2.

Note the one-piece rear wings of this example.

[Photo: Steve Lynch]

The weight saved by using 8.0 mm thick side members was not enough on its own to give the twin steer parity with the trailing-axle chassis, which through its simplicity gave Scania one of the lightest three-axle tractors on the market. To make further gains, Scania switched from the strong but heavy multi-leaf suspension that it favoured for its 6 x 2 layout to a lighter parabolic arrangement for the front and rear axles of twin steer and a hybrid spring/air system for the second steering axle.

As well as saving weight, the air suspension arrangement of the second steering axle allowed the driver to raise it for short periods to gain extra traction. This operation was carried out by depressing a switch mounted in the top right of the dashboard that had to be held down during the procedure, which, unlike the trailing-axle chassis, made empty running with the axle raised an impossibility. *(Photo: Marcus Lester)*

The twin-steer chassis was mainly engineered to meet the changing requirements of UK operators, so Scania Great Britain were the first to market it with a pair of P112 tractors going into service at the end of 1986 with the General Haulage Company of Leeds, which would operate them with both twin and three-axled trailers. However, the chassis would become available throughout Europe later in 1987.

The compact layout utilised a short, for a 6 x 2, 3.8-metre wheelbase. This only allowed room for a 390-litre diesel tank on the right-hand side of the chassis in standard form. As an option, the 300-litre tank seen here was available for the left of the chassis. However, the installation of this item was not straightforward, requiring the re-positioning and re-plumbing of air tanks to accommodate it, which made it cost-prohibitive to some.

The Irish East - West concern was a big 2-series user and quickly adopted the twin-steer chassis in large numbers. *(Photo: Adrian Cypher)*

Taylor's of Martley had been running Scanias since an early pair of LB80s that were purchased in 1973/4. The family firm found the reliability exceptional, which for a company that prided itself on its service was essential. Natural progression soon saw LB81s and then LB111s in the smart green, black and red livery

before 112s, which were operated in both P and R cab format. In the mid and late1980s, the firm's thirty 112 tractors made up around half the strength, such was its suitability for UK general haulage.

Rather than opt for the costly factory modifications for the extra 300-litre diesel tank, Taylor's augmented the

range of this P112 twin steer with a catwalk item. Such work was easily managed by the company's competent workshop, which undertook all servicing, repairs and painting.

Note the wide axle spread of the trailer and tree damage to the top corner. *(Photo: Marcus Lester)*

Although Scania's three-axle chassis gave the company a two-pronged attack on the market and both proved popular, there was still a great deal of demand for the traditional 4 x 2 set-up among UK and European operators. The type's flexibility, running costs, economy and ease of service were just some of the points that made its configuration so attractive.

Andy Vane had this wonderful example working under contract to Laser Transport and it was a young Paul Willis, not long having passed his Class 1, who got to drive it on its regular Manchester Trunk. However, the intrepid Paul hankered after continental work and an opening with Hangartner brought his relationship with D319 MKP, though not Andy Vane, to a premature end after just two weeks.

Note that despite the anti-slip design, black rubber has been laid on the cab steps. This was actually cut from spray-suppression mats. *(Photo: Paul Willis)*

This superb R112M of Naylors Transport provides another fine example of Scania's 4 x 2 chassis in all its beautifully proportioned glory. A 4 x 2 tractor seldom looked more right than an R cabbed unit with the 3.4-metre wheelbase and no air kit.

It would seem that top weight was not a criterion in the case of this combination running at up to 32 tons on four axles, but to weight-conscious operators working with dedicated trailers the 950 kg difference between the twin steer and the 4 x 2 chassis could be an important factor.

Note the Scania badge stuck to the fridge unit of the trailer and the P112 of Salford Van Hire just visible behind. *(Photo: David Wakefield)*

As good as they were, the 4 x 2, 6 x 2 and 6 x 2/4, all designed for 51.2-ton operation, were just not enough truck for operators such as Graham Keedwell who needed to handle 100-ton-plus loads. Scania's stout E chassis was the solution for many in this sector and in standard form was capable of operating at up to 150 tons. The F958 frame of this model carried an internal side member of 8.0 mm thickness in addition to the outer one of 9.5 mm, hence the 958 designation, making for an extremely strong chassis as the base for a tractor or ballasted prime mover. Although the DSC14 05 was the only engine available in UK 142s by this time, it had been the standard engine for this chassis since the introduction of the intercooler in 1983, while the 388 bhp turbo-only engine was an option until it went out of production.

The double-drive rear bogie was made up from a pair of AD100 axles with a capacity of 30,000 kg and utilised single reduction in the axles with hub reduction hubs. Various axle ratios were available to give operators a good mix of performance stretching from a fast 62.4 mph top speed with 1 in 12.3 gradeability at 150 tons GTW to 41.1 mph with 1 in 7.8 gradeability at the same weight. The faster gear set options allowed operators to work competitively at lower weights, too.

Note the cut-down bumper, a unique feature of the E chassis. *(Photo: Clive Davies)*

As one sage operator put it, 'if you employ an elephant to do the work of a horse you will be guaranteed long and reliable service'. Scania's 2-series may have been pricey when compared to its 'on paper' rivals, but the built-in longevity was guaranteed and even if the original purchaser was not planning on running the truck beyond three or five years, this would still be reflected in the residual value of a used 2-series Scania, which always commanded the highest prices on the second-hand market.

Quite apart from still being on active service in 2006, this 19-year-old unit was also working in the hostile environment of the Orkneys when the author encountered it. That the cab had stood up so well to the ravages of the weather and constant salty atmosphere of the islands, was probably due to the improved galvanisation and wax-oil process introduced in 1985.

Note the absence of the Scania badge and that the area underneath, which would normally have been mesh, seems to have been filled in.

(Photos: Author)

At the closing stages of 1987, this photograph would have encapsulated the entire span of Scania's operations in the UK. Ray Hingley's lovingly restored LB76 was the very first example imported and is aptly named 'Swedish Ancestor'. The LB76 was a revelation in the mid-1960s and quickly established a fine reputation, especially for driver comfort. From those early days, Scania nurtured an ever-growing market for its trucks in the UK, which saw many fleets, such as that of A Hingley, moving away from domestic products.

Despite both these trucks representing top-weight tractors of their respective time, the difference in size is quite incredible given the brief fifteen-year period between the designs; even riding on the trailer the LB76 seems minuscule in comparison to the late model R112 here.

Scania considered Hingley's LB76 as very important to its UK history and accordingly included it in the original Roadshow to promote the 2-series in 1981.

(Photo: Adrian Cypher)

Scania announced the 2-series replacement in autumn 1987 with deliveries of the new 3-series trucks appearing the following February. This meant that the last UK 2-series trucks were registered on F-plates, so how did R T Keedwell end up with a G-registered example? The truck was actually an early R113 and the only explanation for the badge would be a replacement grille from an older truck following a minor shunt.

The 2-series had spanned seven years with a staggering 170,158 trucks being produced. To say that the range with its modular system had been a success for Scania would be a massive understatement. *(Photo: Clive Davies)*